The Sharing Economy: Its Pitfalls and Promises

THE SHARING ECONOMY: ITS PITFALLS AND PROMISES

MICHAEL C. MUNGER

Institute of
Economic Affairs

First published in Great Britain in 2021 by
The Institute of Economic Affairs
2 Lord North Street
Westminster
London SW1P 3LB
in association with London Publishing Partnership Ltd
www.londonpublishingpartnership.co.uk

The mission of the Institute of Economic Affairs is to improve understanding of the fundamental institutions of a free society by analysing and expounding the role of markets in solving economic and social problems.

A CIP catalogue record for this book is available from the British Library.

ISBN 978-0-255-36791-2

Many IEA publications are translated into languages other than English or are reprinted. Permission to translate or to reprint should be sought from the Director General at the address above.

Typeset in Kepler by T&T Productions Ltd
www.tandtproductions.com

Printed and bound by Page Bros

CONTENTS

ABOUT THE AUTHOR

Michael Munger is a researcher and administrator at Duke University in North Carolina. He is a senior research fellow at the Independent Institute in Oakland, California, and at the American Institute for Economic Research at Great Barrington, Massachusetts. He has taught at Dartmouth College, the University of Texas, and the University of North Carolina. His published research has covered spatial theory, political decision-making and the problem of voluntary exchange. His most recent book, *Is Capitalism Sustainable?*, was published in 2019 by the American Institute for Economic Research. He is a past editor of the journal *Public Choice*, as well as a past president of the Public Choice Society. His first professional position was as a staff economist at the US Federal Trade Commission. He received his PhD in economics at Washington University in 1984.

ACKNOWLEDGEMENTS

This project was suggested by Jamie Whyte, and was re-worked by Richard Wellings, both of the IEA. My thanks to them for the proposal, and to Syed Kamall, also of the IEA, for seeing things through, when there were many competing demands on his time and resources. Thanks are due to Curtis Bram for research assistance; thanks also to Jon Wainwright for converting the manuscript into something resembling workable prose. Numerous helpful suggestions and improvements were suggested by Drew Millard. All of those who deserve credit for what is done well here are blameless for what is done poorly; for that, I am solely responsible.

The ideas expressed here owe credit, but no blame, to seminar participants at the University of Colorado, Oklahoma State University, the University of Texas, and Trinity College in the US, as well as the Institute for Liberal Studies in Canada, and the ANU and Notre Dame in Australia. Finally, thanks to Donna Gingerella for tolerating my need to spend far longer than was plausible working on the details herein.

SUMMARY

- Platforms are institutions that solve the problems of
  delivering a good or service, of clearing payments, and
  of creating trust between buyer and seller.
- In the past two decades, the physical locations in
  which transactions take place, such as the city market
  or shopping centre, have increasingly been replaced
  by online platforms. The platform revolution is an
  economic revolution as momentous as the Neolithic
  and Industrial Revolutions.
- The platform revolution is delivering reductions in the
  transaction costs of renting. New and different ways
  of partitioning short-term ownership have emerged.
  The shared feature of these markets is that they enable
  profitable means of commodifying excess capacity
  that until now could only be wasted. We pay for
  storage twice: wasted space, and forgone capital value.
- The platform economy is making more intensive and
  efficient use of resources that are otherwise idle. In the
  long run, the consequence will be a sharp increase in
  the durability and average life of those resources as
  they are replaced.
- By monetising the deadweight loss of queuing, new
  software platforms are capturing much of the value

that would previously have been wasted by the friction of transaction costs.

- Entrepreneurs can now move far beyond aspiring only to sell products or services. They can sell reductions in transaction costs alone.

- Services such as Uber are software platforms which make possible transactions that otherwise could not take place. Uber is a disruptive technology which sells reductions in transaction costs, enabling a wide variety of peer-to-peer exchanges and arrangements.

- The platform economy is making products and services that once did not exist, or were available only to the wealthy, available universally and practically free of charge.

- Some new software platforms are being prohibited by regulators precisely because they work better and disrupt the existing systems of cronyism. Regulators who place restrictions on services such as Airbnb typically ignore the real price signal being sent by the creation of the new platforms, which is that supply is being restricted. The correct solution is to set housing free to expand residential options.

- Regulators must embrace permissionless innovation, adopting a strong presumption in favour of allowing experimentation with new technologies and new business platforms.

- On the other hand, regulators must avoid outdated thinking about antitrust policy as focusing on market structure. Platforms, by their nature, are giants. Any platform is by definition a monopoly within its own boundaries; in fact that is the advantage of platforms. The new regulatory framework must focus on limiting the power of platforms, especially their political power, rather than forcing inefficiency and waste by restricting their size.

FIGURES

1 INTRODUCTION

This book addresses some recent changes in a variety of markets and business activities. The core argument is that more and more markets are 'two-sided', with consumers and sellers both actively seeking ways to transact. A common way to characterise two-sided markets is 'peer-to-peer'; the reason this is important is that two-sided markets are different from the traditional 'price-taking behaviour' models used in textbook economics. At the time this book is going to press, the global Covid-19 pandemic has given this transformation a new urgency.

The 'place' where many transactions occur was once physical, such as at a city market or a mall. But in the past two decades these physical locations have increasingly been replaced by virtual domains called 'online platforms'.

One of the first attempts to model this phenomenon was Rochet and Tirole (2003: 990). As they put it:

> Buyers of video game consoles want games to play on; game developers pick platforms that are or will be popular among gamers. Cardholders value credit or debit cards only to the extent that these are accepted by the merchants they patronize; affiliated merchants benefit

from a widespread diffusion of cards among consumers. More generally, many if not most markets with network externalities are characterized by the presence of two distinct sides whose ultimate benefit stems from interacting through a common platform.

I will argue that platforms should be thought of as selling reductions in 'transaction costs', or the costs of organising and consummating an exchange, rental or other market action.[1] The three aspects of transaction costs that are relevant to online platforms are *triangulation* (finding information and other parties to transact with), *transfer* (the delivery of the product or service, and making the payment), and *trust* (the ability to rely on the terms of the agreement without resort to external enforcement).

In this setting, much of the action in exchange is 'peer-to-peer'. Owners and potential users of durables such as cars or flats find ways to share, with the transactions looking like rentals. The value of these exchanges, taken individually, is small, and can be blocked by transaction costs. Platforms act as matchmakers, or middlemen, a role that traders have taken since their very first exchanges thousands of years ago. The difference now is that the matchmakers are selling only reductions in transaction costs

---

1   One of the most general definitions of 'transaction costs' was given by Douglass North (1992), who described four components: measuring (by unit, by weight, or by period of time), enforcement (ensuring honesty and compliance with contractual obligations), ideology (attitudes toward the transaction), and 'the size of the market' (problems of scale, as well as transportation).

and often have no direct role in buying or selling anything; they just help buyers and sellers in two-sided markets find each other and transact. This is quite different from the way that manufacturers are often conceived in academic economics (Evans and Schmalensee 2016: 2):

> Traditional manufacturing businesses, for instance, buy raw materials, make stuff, and sell that stuff to customers. But matchmakers' raw materials are the different groups of customers that they help bring together, not anything that they buy at all. And part of the stuff they sell to members of each group is access to members of the other groups. All of them operate physical or virtual places where members of these different groups get together. For this reason, they are often called *multisided platforms*. They're places where all of these different groups can meet [emphasis added].

Platforms have always been with us, as a means of reducing transaction costs. But the dramatic increase in the importance of platforms in the last two decades is revolutionary.

3

2   REVOLUTIONS AND DISRUPTION

Economic revolutions do not care what we think of them. For people who believe they are the centre of the universe, or for technocrats who want to pull strings and push levers to 'run things', that can be very disquieting. But failing to understand that economies are organic complex systems can cause problems that make things much worse. These systems have internal dynamics that operate independently of the will of the state, or of any individual for that matter.[1] This book is an attempt to explain the dynamics of the complex systems called 'platforms' and to explain why, when platforms are working properly, we never notice problems in the first place.

We face the intersection of two great sources of turmoil for markets and society: the constant conflict over the degree of state direction of the economy, and the profoundly disruptive effect of the new 'platform economy'. Either of these alone would make for disquieting politics; together,

---

1   'Complex systems' in economics consist of sets of interacting individuals who may not be fully aware of their mutual dependence – who update their actions and strategies in response to the outcome they mutually create but that none may intend. This definition is given in Arthur (1999), but it is consistent with Hayek's (1988) notion of the 'extended order'.

they have the potential for wrenching and unpredictable change. In a recent article, Littlewood (2018: 444) tried to peer at least a little way into the future:

> It is not often that I quote with approval the words of Tony Benn, the erstwhile leader of the Labour left. His vision of a socialist Britain failed in his lifetime, but as he said, 'Every generation has to fight the same battles again and again for there is no final victory and no final defeat'.
>
> He was right: the identical argument applies to the struggle for free markets. In a democracy the battle of ideas is never over. The triumphalism following the Thatcher and Reagan years and the fall of the Berlin Wall was misplaced: it turns out that the intellectual advance of market liberalism in the 1980s was not some permanent Galileo-like discovery changing human understanding in perpetuity. It was merely a protracted skirmish which is now being re-enacted, not necessarily, on this occasion, to the advantage of those of us who favour free markets.
>
> To win this clash of ideologies for a second time, free market proponents need to recalibrate the ammunition they are deploying. Simply stating that arguments about the market were addressed and resolved several decades ago will not persuade a new generation that big advances in state power are deeply undesirable.

No final victory; no final defeat. Policy reactions to the dynamism of market capitalism and democratic politics require agility in tactics and nimbleness of mind. This book considers some of the implications, problems and promises of the new platform economy, and tries to make some recommendations for the future, such as it can be seen.

But the difficulties that we are facing have some important precursors. The (probably apocryphal) story is told that one Ned Ludd, an apprentice weaver from Leicester, smashed two knitting frames after having been abused – the abuse may have been a whipping by his master, or it may have been mocking by local youths. But, in any case, the apprentice's petulance was elevated to militancy and sacrifice by Lord Byron in his 1816 'Song for the Luddites':

> As the liberty lads o'er the sea
> Bought their freedom, and cheaply, with blood,
> So we, boys, we
> Shall die fighting or live free,
> And down with all kings but King Ludd!

Byron, by romanticising the Ludd myth, was reflecting a widely shared impulse to delay or impede – by violence if necessary – the kinds of changes that economists now call 'creative destruction'. By 1810, the followers of 'King Ludd' were active in many parts of England, so active in fact that the British government deployed more troops against domestic revolution than it sent to face Napoleon in Spain.

One imagines an analogous movement, sparked by one Ur Ludd, about 8,000 years ago, when someone started to poke at the ground with a sharp stick, fashioning a hole in the loosened earth in which to plant seeds. Ur Ludd is likely to have broken the stick and kicked the seeds about, hoping to fend off the move to fixed agriculture and preserve the hunter-gatherer lifestyle. All the customs, all the ways of making a living and a life, that Ur Ludd – and Ned Ludd – knew, were bound up in an older way of doing things. The 'old way' was very different, with hunter-gatherer clans for Ur and rural semi-feudal fixed agriculture for Ned, but to the extent that they thought violence might delay change, they were happy to riot.

Of course, *real* violence – focused and effective violence – typically relies on the active complicity of the state. The current apostles of King Ludd find ready allies in the halls of Congress, Parliament and especially in local government. With hindsight, we can see that the opponents of the Neolithic and the Industrial Revolutions were doomed to fail. But those battles were never really won and never really lost. Both revolutions corroded the cultural and economic habits that people had taken for granted for centuries. Both changed life for the worse, at least at first and for some people.[2] But they happened, and before long, life started to get better.

---

2   Yuval Harari called the switch from nomadic to agricultural life 'history's biggest fraud'. He argued that 'Rather than heralding a new era of easy living, the Agricultural Revolution left farmers with lives generally more difficult and less satisfying than those of foragers. Hunter-gatherers spent their time in more stimulating and varied ways, and were less in danger of starvation and disease. The Agricultural Revolution certainly enlarged the sum total of food at the disposal of humankind, but the extra food did not translate into a better diet or more leisure. Rather, it translated into population explosions and pampered elites. The average farmer worked harder than the average forager, and got a worse diet in return' (Harari 2015: 79).

The new revolution, the 'platform revolution', is having its first effects right now, all around us. It will be enormously destructive. In many ways, it will change life for the worse, at least at first and for some people. But it is going to happen, because this economic revolution, like its predecessors, does not care what we think of it. The revolution is happening because the economic logic is ineluctable. The purpose of this book is to explain what is happening, so that we can position ourselves to enjoy the benefits sooner, and perhaps mitigate some of the problems.

Transaction costs and commodifying excess capacity

In the early 1930s, while just beginning his work as an economist at what is now the University of Dundee, Ronald Coase travelled to the US and interviewed a number of corporate CEOs. Coase focused on a deceptively simple question: economists talk about the value of prices and decentralised markets in organising cooperative human behaviour, but if markets are so great, why are there firms?

After all, no one comes home at the end of a hard day and says, 'Holy cow, *prices* were in such a bad mood today!' Instead, they say that their *boss*, an actual human, was in a bad mood. Workers do not receive signals from prices; they get orders from bosses. Firms developed in order to bypass the market mechanism, because using prices and markets can be 'expensive'. The kinds of expense that Coase (1937) identified were dubbed 'transaction costs'.

Prices guide economic activity at some level, both in terms of the opportunity cost of commodities – someone else will pay more than the value of the use I envision for the thing – and in terms of the 'profit test', which forces firms to consider whether their actions are socially valuable. But at the level of day-to-day activity, prices never speak directly to most of us.

Imagine that I work on a production line, adding two screws to the wiring connectors on an appliance. I do not go to eBay to sell the incomplete frame, although I could. What happens instead is that the conveyor moves the appliance chassis to the next person on the production line, who attaches a cover on the motor housing, and so on, down the line. The next workers respond to the orders of the foreman, who decides which station on the line each person will occupy that day.

For those who favour planning of the entire economy, of course, this seems to suggest that it is a mistake to use markets at all; nations should be one big firm, as many socialists have been telling us all along. But that is not right, either. Prices and market processes really do make it possible to organise large groups of people across great distances, and with no central direction or personal knowledge of what other people are doing. Prices, the division of labour and market systems allow humans to cooperate better, and to have more stuff to use, to wear, to eat, or to play with than any other system. Without the division of labour, the creation of wealth and prosperity is limited, and can only be enjoyed by elites. As Adam Smith [1776] (1981) famously pointed out, 'division of labour is limited by the extent of the market', so that the larger the number of entities trading in a market system, the greater the division of labour, and the greater the wealth to be shared.

Owning, renting and the commodification of excess capacity

Coase's observations about transaction costs are vitally important. As I previously argued (Munger 2015), if Coase were alive today he would ask, 'Why do we own things, instead of sharing them in common, or renting them?' The remarkable thing is that this 'different question' has the same answer: transaction costs.

To see why, remember that the convention or norm of exclusive private ownership is a notable feature of human development. Over thousands of years, in myriad settings, the view became accepted that having an 'owner' of a piece of land or a tool or a firm was better than having those things owned in common. Why would that be? After all, Rousseau [1754] (1984) famously argued:

> The first man, who after enclosing a piece of ground, took it into his head to say, this is mine; and found people simple enough to believe him, was the real founder of civil society. How many crimes, how many wars, how many murders, how many misfortunes and honours, might not anyone have saved the human species, who pulling up the stakes or filling up the ditches should have cried to his fellows: Beware of listening to this impostor; you are lost, if you forget that *the fruits*

of the earth belong equally to us all, and the earth itself
to nobody [emphasis added].

Today, it is now widely recognised that Rousseau's romantic assessment actually leads to catastrophe, the 'tragedy of the commons'. But the idea of sharing is attractive, both because it's cheaper and because human nature is cooperative. It turns out that private cooperative division of access can work, and that platforms can make it possible.

An owner of a secure property right can plan for the future and steward the resource or capital asset. The right of an ownership claim also gives the owner residual and presumptive rights of control, giving both incentives and capacity to ensure action is taken when contracts are silent or incompletely specified, or are breached by other parties. The owner or holder of these residual rights can therefore act unilaterally, without asking permission or having to negotiate contracts for use of the owned resource.[3]

Uncertainty and friction in getting things done are central facts of life in any economy, so Rousseau was just wrong about the imaginary advantages of a system where 'the fruits of the earth belong to all'. Private ownership is here to stay, in any system that works. But the distribution and exchange of contracts in how things will be used is a different question. In this book, I will use the word 'sharing' in the way that has become increasingly common in a variety

---

3   The importance of these rights, and the convention of ownership, has been remarked on variously by many theorists. A diverse sampling would include Hume (1740), Demsetz (1967), Hardin (1968), Williamson (1975, 1985), Barzel (1989) and Libecap (1989).

of applications and new businesses such as Uber, Airbnb and BlaBlaCar. The underlying asset being shared, through renting or some other process, is privately owned, and the interests of the residual rights holder are operating in the background. But the reduction in transaction costs implied by the new system fosters the *commodification* of excess capacity, to the point where the *use* of the asset can be bought and sold separately from the underlying rights of ownership.

In effect, as every first-year law student learns in the 'Introduction to Contracts' class, ownership implies a bundle of rights. Some of these rights can be shared, or rented out, and others are retained by the primary residual claims owner. That is why having a job and 'renting out' one's labour is not slavery; that is why I get to stay in an Airbnb for two nights and have exclusive use of the flat during that time, but the owner retains all the rights (and responsibilities) of the residual claims holder.

So, why do we own, rather than rent? The answer is that, until recently, renting out – sharing the 'temporary use rights' portion of the property bundle – has been associated with transaction costs that overwhelm the revenue that could be earned through commodification. But that is not obviously, or definitionally, true. The 'sharing economy' is a wide assortment of apparently different ways of partitioning short-term ownership; the shared feature of these markets is that they enable profitable means of commodifying excess capacity that until now could only be wasted, or at best stored.

The choice of renting or owning, or occupying some hybrid form, is of course not solely driven by general market conditions. The most important economic element of 'durables' is time. That is, we don't want the thing itself as much as we want the stream of services or value we associate with the thing. I don't want a hammer; what I want is to have these nails driven into a wall in just the place I want and at whatever time I might want it. As a result, I own the hammer myself and keep it in a toolbox, taking up space in my closet.

On a broader scale, I want living space and I want substantial control over that space's security, temperature, lighting and location. I can obtain those things by *owning* the space; alternatively, I can obtain those things by renting, signing a contract that leaves residual control rights (and responsibility for normal repairs and upkeep) in the hands of the landlord.

The relative preference for renting versus owning 'housing services' varies across people and over time. But the cost, including the transaction cost, of each of the two choices also matters. The ability to borrow, the prospect of being able to sell the property, and the security of the neighbourhood are of great importance. Housing is not a commodity, like soybeans or pork bellies. Every residence is a local monopoly. The ownership of housing gives one greater control, and greater rights to the appreciation of the value of the property, but also comes with the responsibility for maintenance and repair, and the risk of capital loss if prices fall.

There are substantial changes over time in the way people make this choice. As an example, consider the pattern of housing tenancy in England (Figure 1). The 'social renters' are perhaps a different category, as they are recipients of a state-sponsored subsidy. But of the private housing sector, the figure illustrates a substantial, perhaps even surprising, change in the modality of securing housing services over time. In 1920 more than three-quarters of English citizens lived in housing that was formally owned by someone else; by 1980 that figure had fallen to just over 5 per cent. Conversely, in 1920 only about a quarter of English citizens owned the homes they lived in; since the late 1970s, this proportion has consistently been more like two-thirds of the total.

Figure 1   Housing by tenure in England: 1918–2019

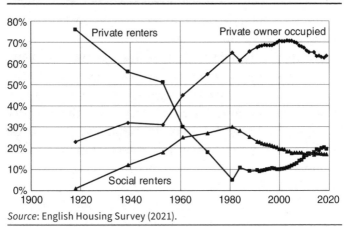

Source: English Housing Survey (2021).

If I am right that Coase's question would be 'Why do people own, rather than rent?' and that his answer would be 'transaction costs', then what changed over the past century? There is a strong norm, dating at least back to Nobel economist Gary Becker, against reasoning from preference changes as explanations for such wide swings in consumption patterns. Still, it is quite possible that people in the UK now simply want to own more than was once the case. Schoenauer (2003: 344–46) called this 'domestic revival'.

But the more likely causes can be inferred from the standard economic variables of changes in relative prices, changes in incomes, and changes in institutional arrangements. As is detailed in Lomax and Callen (1990), reliance on mortgages from building societies in the first half of the twentieth century raised a variety of costs, some of them monetary but many taking the form of transaction costs – paperwork, inspections, difficulty in obtaining permissions, and a lack of responsiveness to market forces – that made buying a home difficult.

Changes in the financial industry, reducing the nominal and effective price of home ownership, as well as increases in family income, have spurred a dramatic reversal in the dominant form of 'consumption' of housing flows, by changing the ownership structure of the housing stock, as Figure 1 illustrates. Nonetheless, just as there was nothing permanent about the distribution of ownership–rental patterns of 1910, this could all change again. The prices, and associated risks, of owning land and buildings are substantial in many parts of the UK. Cheaper and more effective systems of renting could tip the own–rent distribution back in the other direction.

According to the Local Government Association (2019), 23-year-olds born in 1996 are half as likely to own homes as those born in 1976 at the same age. Furthermore, substantial proportions of current owners feel stuck, unable to sell their homes and wishing they could divest themselves of maintenance costs and the risk of financial loss.

This reveals the power of the Coasian analysis: the dividing line between one pattern of consumption, or production, and another may not be the sorts of costs economists can write down in supply and demand curves. The relevant costs may be transaction costs, and significant transformations in institutional arrangements, based on platforms, can change everything in surprisingly short order. The reason people own consumer durables such as cars, houses, suits, shoes and stand mixers is that owning, maintaining and storing happens to be the most convenient way to assure immediate and reliable access to that thing. That is remarkable and frankly wasteful.

We have to pay for everything *twice*: first in the value of the capital tied up in something that we rarely use, which just sits around gathering dust; and second for the cost of the space of storing the stuff securely, under lock and key, to keep other people from using it, while it depreciates in value. According to the Self-Storage Association (SSA),[4] there are nearly 1,500 self-storage sites in the UK, offering more than 42 million square feet of space for unused stuff. The total revenue of the industry, as reported by the SSA, was well over half a billion pounds in 2016.

---

4   Size of the industry. Self Storage Association (https://www.ssauk.com/industry-info/size-of-the-industry/). Interestingly, according to the SSA the self-storage industry, in the formal sense of large specialised units with locks available for rental, originated in London in 1979. The London origin and rapid growth of these services presaged the rapid growth of rents for even the tiniest flats in the London market. See also Cohen (2018) for background.

What is it that is being 'stored'? The word itself suggests the answer: 'store' comes from Old French, through Middle English, originating with the Latin verb 'instaurare', which means to 'renew'. If I have a piece of cake, and eat it, it's gone. If I have a power drill, and use it, then store it, it is 'renewed'. Storage means I can use my drill and have it, too. Consequently, we store stuff, so we can 'renew' our use of it in the future. In the West, we store bicycles, furniture, appliances and electronics in garages and rental spaces that are safer, more solidly constructed, cleaner and more comfortable than the median *human* habitation in many developing nations.

Cost in two-sided markets: who is buying and who is selling?

Defining 'cost', particularly marginal cost, has long been a vexing problem for economics. Many externalities, for example, are defined with respect to a divergence between private and social marginal costs for an activity. The technical problem has been made far more complex, but more important and technically more interesting, by the recent transformation of many production and exchange relationships by the emergence of the 'platform economy', which I take (primarily) to mean the commodification of excess capacity and the reduction of transaction costs in two-sided markets.

It is unsurprising that the platform economy has disrupted the structure of manufacturing and retail business, from Amazon to Zillow. The fifteen largest publicly traded platform firms globally already have more than £200 billion in market capitalisation (Statista 2021), and the fastest-growing firms globally have platform business models (Parker et al. 2016: 3). Continued improvements in cloud computing, the 'Internet of Things', and mobile devices enable the extension of platforms into increasing numbers of markets as well as the creation of new markets.

But perhaps the most disruptive facet of the platform revolution has been what some call the 'sharing economy', where the difference between consumer and producer/seller is blurred. Commodification of excess capacity introduces an opportunity cost of storage and unused productive function. One obvious example is Airbnb, which softens the 'peak load' constraint on total rental housing available in a location. In a period of a festival or sporting event, such as the Olympics, a large of number of consumer/owners of housing services become renters of housing services, leaving town for a week or more while someone pays a high price to rent their flat. These 'peer to peer' or 'two-sided' markets require mediation or brokering to reduce transaction costs, but given the profits available for platforms that can solve the problem the trend is likely to accelerate (Frenken and Schor 2017; Frenken et al. 2015). This 'bottom line' is actually simple: platform-induced reduction in transaction costs enables a rental market for excess capacity to emerge, generating gains from trade. The ability to monetise excess capacity may also induce some renters to become owners of the asset.

Figure 2 shows the number of individuals in the US aged 18 and over who have used, and are forecast to use, a community-based online service that coordinates peer-to-peer paid access to property, goods and services, in total and as a percentage of the US population. The point is that direct participation in buying and selling online has gone from less than 10 per cent to nearly 30 per cent of the population in less than a decade. What changed?

Figure 2   Sharing economy users and US population

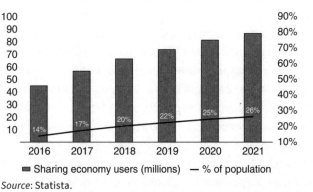

Source: Statista.

The answer is 'transaction costs', with the explosion of digital platforms. In his 1937 *Economica* paper, R. H. Coase famously asked a difficult question: if markets and prices are so effective for value creation, why do firms exist? His answer was 'transaction costs', meaning that using the price system and contracts was expensive. Firms organise production lines as small, self-contained 'command economies'; each firm expands or shrinks as variations in transaction costs move the margin at which the last transaction organised internally costs as much as the next transaction organised through markets and prices, or it can buy the input or service in the market, sometimes quite quickly, as innovations in informing, transacting and enforcing agreements emerge (Williamson 1981; Klein 2005).

The platform economy operates on a nearly identical logic, but on a different margin. Instead of 'make or buy', the relevant choice for buyers is 'own or share;' for owners, the choice is 'store or share'. Many durable assets, ranging from clothing to kitchen equipment, and from lawn mowers to electricity generation facilities, sit idle for much, and likely most, of their useful lives. Digital platform markets make excess capacity economically relevant by increasing the opportunity cost of idleness. Each unused minute involves both storage costs and the opportunity cost rate of return that the durable asset's owner could be earning on excess capacity.

But if the transaction costs of commodifying excess capacity are expensive, there are no buyers or sellers, because either (a) durables are simply something we pay to store, rather than something we imagine could produce revenue, or (b) durables are things we might forgo owning entirely and simply rent when we need them.

Platforms that reduce the transaction costs of such market participants enable peer-to-peer exchanges that are immediate and dynamic. Until now, we have had no means of pricing the forgone use of excess capacity. But the platform economy simultaneously prices the opportunity cost and provides an outlet by which even very temporary excess capacity can be bought and sold with very little friction.

There is an interesting parallel here to a famous disagreement in price theory, pitting Meade (1952) against Cheung (1973). Meade recognised that there was a complex 'joint production' between bees and fruit trees, with the marginal costs of fruit production dependent on the presence of bees to pollinate the flowers from which fruit would grow. Meade (1952: 57) claimed that the price mechanism could not handle this problem, at least not efficiently:

> [T]he apple-farmer provides to the beekeeper some of his factors free of charge. The apple-farmer is paid less than the value of his marginal social net product, and the bee-keeper receives more than the value of his marginal social net product.

Twenty years later, Steven Cheung investigated the economic institutions surrounding the provision of fruit trees with pollination services, and discovered that the problem had in fact been solved rather neatly, with a 'custom of the orchards' that in effect required that each farmer contract with a number of bees sufficient to pollinate, on average, the quantity of fruit trees that farmer owned. This meant that while Meade was right that the exact location of the trees being pollinated was unclear – bees don't recognise property lines – the average solution was approximately correct and the market functioned reasonably well without coercive subsidies.

More important, for our purposes, the value of the honey produced differs substantially depending on the type of flower being pollinated. Remarkably, the price of the service, and for that matter the 'direction' of the notion of the service itself, depends rather precisely on this value. In two-sided markets, it may not be clear just who is the buyer, and who is the seller, because what platforms foster is cooperation.

In the case of the bees (described by Munger 2007), almonds in California need to be pollinated, but almond honey is not very palatable and in any case the amount of honey produced is negligible. Consequently, in California almond growers pay beekeepers to provide pollination. But in Florida orange blossoms produce delicious, fragrant honey. And orange blossom nectar is plentiful and sweet; the result is that in Florida beekeepers pay orange farmers for the right to park their hives in the groves. The same 'service' *actually reverses direction* in terms of the net benefits to the participants, and the price system calibrates the marginal value and charges the relatively greater-benefiting party. But the price in either case is less than it would be if the service lacked the feature of shared production that had originally caught Meade's attention.

I expect that fifty years from now people will look back on this era and be amazed at all the waste. Why do we pay for everything twice, once to buy it and then again to store it? Even a purely selfish person should realise that it would be more rational, and actually cheaper, to devise ways to share, because renting is cheaper than owning and then all the users in effect *share* the storage costs. Instead of closets and garages and parking spaces clogging busy city streets, we could actually use that space, for people, for doing things.[5]

The answer is surprisingly simple: what looks like selfishness is just a consequence of transaction costs. We have stuff, and we store stuff, because doing anything else is more trouble than it's worth. If I own something, I control it. If I want to rent, or borrow that thing, I am much more dependent on other people. They may break it, or fail to return it, and, besides, what if I want it right now and someone else has it?

Nonetheless, unless one is a miser or Tolkien's dragon Smaug, most people don't fundamentally want *stuff*. What they want is the *stream of services* that stuff provides, over time. So, if people *own* stuff – clothes, tools, cars, houses – rather than *rent*, it is because owning renews access to those services more reliably and at lower cost than renting. The important thing to recognise is that this preference for owning is not an essential part of human nature. It could change quickly, if entrepreneurs can work out ways to *sell reductions in transaction costs*. We only own stuff if the transaction cost of sharing is high. But traditional notions of a buyer, and a seller, will often be blurred, because these transactions will increasingly be consummated on platforms.

---

5   The costs of regulations mandating minimum parking requirements for new housing are enormously expensive and fall disproportionately on the poor and middle class (Seibert 2008). And the potential gains from repurposing all that essentially wasted storage space are one of the most optimistic aspects of current city planning (Berg 2016).

3 PLATFORMS AND OWNERSHIP

The entrepreneurs of the new economy are focused on making profits, just as entrepreneurs have always been. But for the first time in human history, entrepreneurs can dispense with selling products or services, and sell reductions in transaction costs alone. The important thing to recognise is that, from the perspective of buyers, consumers and users, *all* costs are transaction costs. The total costs of using or owning a thing are dependent on the particular circumstances of time and place for that commodity and that transaction. Economists often say, 'Demand curves slope downward', meaning that price cuts lead to more sales. But for consumers, the 'price' is the sum of the monetary cost and the costs of inconvenience and queuing. So a seller can also sell more by lowering transaction costs.

It is tempting to define transaction costs as all the costs of completing a transaction other than the costs of producing the good or service being sold, but even that is too simple. The notion of separating the good itself from the way that it is produced or sold requires ownership, but what most people want is the service the durable good provides. If entrepreneurship is now refocused on providing brief access to the *services* of the good but not ownership of the good itself, the whole notion of 'cost' is confused.

What is clear is that cutting the cost, either monetary costs or inconvenience of use, means, firstly, that people will *buy more* and, secondly, that *more people* will buy. It is easy to forget that many items, from cars to refrigerators, and from televisions to mobile phones, were at first only toys for the very rich. Producing these products at scale allowed prices to come down, quality to increase and access to the product to be expanded to the entire population. But the actual cost on the price tag is only part of the story. If you can make the product more reliable, easier to use, easier to obtain, easier to find, or otherwise easier to buy, on any margin, you expand the number of people who can use that product.

Several Nobel Prize winners in economics, including Ronald Coase, Eugene Fama, Douglass North, George Stigler and Oliver Williamson, understood transaction costs as forces that blocked transactions more generally. This understanding was developed further in the literature of such scholars as Armen Alchian, Yoram Barzel, Steven N. S. Cheung and Harold Demsetz.[1]

The problem of transaction costs provides the key reason why entrepreneurship is so important: all over the world, 'stuff' is in the wrong place. That is why people exchange: I want something you have more than you want it,

---

and you want something I have more than I want it. If we exchange, we will both be better off, with the same amount of stuff. Why is stuff in the wrong place? The answer is *transaction costs*.

We might call these entrepreneurs, selling reductions in transaction costs, the 'middlemen' in the platform economy. The reason that the platform economy is different is that many of the transactions that take place are actually 'peer-to-peer', meaning that buyers and sellers simply use the platform to find each other, but negotiate and transact on their own. The platform seamlessly solves the problems of transaction costs that might otherwise prevent the exchange from taking place. To succeed, a platform middleman has to find a way to sell, literally to make money from, the reduction in three key categories of transaction costs:

- Triangulation: information about identity and location.
- Transfer: a way of transferring payment and goods that is immediate and as invisible as possible.
- Trust: a way of outsourcing assurance of honesty, and performance of the terms of the contract.

Any system that solves these three problems and facilitates exchange by other people is a 'platform'. Platforms have always been with us, since the very dawn of civilisation, in ancient Sumer, in the city of Ur, in the large markets called the souk or bazaar. Without understanding that platforms are necessary to solve the three transaction cost problems, it is hard to understand why these large markets emerged and were popular. Suppose you have worked for a year, and the result is thirty bags of wheat. You do not have much of a farm, because seeds were not very productive and there were few tools. So thirty bags of wheat is all you have got, and you need to exchange them for things you really need.

You are ten miles outside town. It would seem like the last thing you would want to do is carry that heavy grain to a place where many other grain sellers – competitors – are also selling their grain. You are going to lose because of the competition. Why do you not go way out into the country, in the middle of a field, and sell it there? The answer is: you would be in that field for a long time. Nobody knows that you are there with your thirty sacks of grain.

The souk is a platform. Buyers and sellers can find each other and they can agree on a price, because there are many buyers and many sellers. There is a way to deliver the goods, because everyone pays for their own transport to the souk, and then long-distance transport is facilitated by bundling all the products to be shipped into a caravan, which can be managed and defended more cheaply than many separate shipments. And we trust each other, in at least a limited way, because there are opportunities for reputation and repeat business, and the rudimentary state provides security along the main roads and in this concentrated area. So, we have triangulation, transfer and trust, bundled in the souk. That is why people would go to a souk and not somewhere else.

That kind of market arrangement has existed for thousands of years. In the 1970s and 1980s we might have called a similar arrangement a 'mall', a place where consumers could go and be confident that they could find, pay for, and take delivery of many diverse products and services, and do so safely and with little fear of being cheated or robbed. But before that in the US, for several decades, an obvious example of a platform was the Sears catalogue. In the UK, people of a certain age may recall the British equivalent: Littlewoods Mail Order, established in 1932. The Littlewoods catalogue, published by Sir John Moores, was immediately successful as the key mail-order platform in Great Britain.[2]

Littlewoods, Sears and other mail-order merchants were not selling stuff; each was selling reductions in transaction costs, in the three categories: triangulation, transfer and trust. The catalogue made something closer to peer-to-peer selling possible, with Sears acting as middleman to reduce transaction costs. Suppose it is 1920 and you live in a small town in southern Illinois. There is a train that passes by on a railway now and then, but it does not stop. The only place you can buy stuff is at the town dry goods store, or maybe there is also a seed, feed and hardware store and they have a few dozen simple tools and implements.

---

2   The motto of the Littlewoods catalogue is perhaps the best short summary of the business model of the 'middleman' ever written (https://www.vintagecatalogues.com/home-page):

> We hoist our Flag in the Port of Supply, and right away we sail to the Ports of Demand—the Homes of the People. We intend to help the homely folk of this country, help them to obtain some of the profits made by manufacturing and trading ... to save money on things they must have. This Catalogue is our Ship ... staffed by an All-British crew ... You won't find sleepy, old-fashioned goods carried in the LITTLEWOODS ship. Only the newest of the new goods—honest, British-made merchandise.

That would be what Adam Smith called 'the extent of the market'; that is the cooperation horizon in your world. Not much specialisation, or division of labour, is possible, because the transaction costs are too high. But out in the wide world, division of labour is exploding, both in the diversity of products and the economies of scale in mass producing consumer products. Is there a way to deliver access to this huge, diversified market to your small town? Well, yes, because twice a year this enormous 800-page analogue platform arrives in your mailbox – the printed paper catalogue from Sears, or whatever mail-order company served your home. There were, by 1897, more than 70,000 different products listed for sale, some of them so specialised that the producer probably could not have survived without access to a national market. But the catalogues created that access.

Some of these tens of thousands of products were made by the seller. A few more were purchased and sold under contract by Sears. But a lot of them were just third-party items, made by producers to whom Sears sold space in its paper souk. The catalogue solved the triangulation problem because people could find products they did not even know existed, but now wanted to wear or use on the farm. The clothing was much more beautiful and fashionable than anything that a local seamstress or tailor could have provided.

Sears handled transfer as well. In fact, Sears specialised in reducing the costs of delivery and payment. Much of what Sears did was provide credit to people who had problems annually of coming up with enough money at the right time, so Sears would loan money and then process the payments. The seller would get paid up front by Sears, which would act as intermediary waiting for all the buyer's payments. As for trust, Sears gave an implicit guarantee. If the product didn't work, they would refund it; if it arrived broken, Sears would take care of it. What that meant was that the Sears catalogue and the services behind it were a self-contained platform. Interestingly, once the Sears catalogue became a known commodity as a platform, the space of the platform changed over time to many bricks-and-mortar stores. The Sears store was a smaller-scale (though only slightly smaller; many Sears had products to cover more than 20,000 square metres of space!) version of the catalogue. And the leading Sears brands, such as Craftsman and Kenmore, became revered in their own right for quality and low-cost service (Emmett and Jeuck 1965).

There is another company, one we have all heard of, that updated and dramatically extended the Sears catalogue platform model. That company is Amazon. Amazon once sold nothing but books; in fact, in 1997 when Amazon launched its website, it had a plain but informative banner: 'Earth's Biggest Bookstore'. If division of labour is limited by the extent of the market, Amazon recognised from the outset that the only limit on internet sales was being on Earth.

Just two decades later, you can still buy books from Amazon, but Amazon is the Sears catalogue of the twenty-first century. Because almost everything that Amazon sells is manufactured by someone else. Amazon makes much of its profit from renting 'space', using the software called Amazon Web Services (AWS).[3] Amazon is a platform: I can find the product; I can identify price; I can search across different sellers very easily because Amazon is set up for these searches; I can arrange the payments, because I am actually paying Amazon and then Amazon pays the seller. Amazon is an intermediary protecting me from credit card fraud, taking the risk of fraudulent activity because it can spread the costs out over so many transactions.

Finally, Amazon has an elaborate and highly efficient delivery system. It is automating many of the stages of handling the products between the producer and the consumer. In the present environment, with a premium on social distancing and delivery because of the coronavirus pandemic, the advantages of a 'virtual' instead of a physical mall are obvious. Since Amazon also handles financing and returns, the global pandemic is likely to be the final nail in the coffin of bricks-and-mortar department stores.

The point is that the three aspects of transaction costs – triangulation, transfer and trust – are all handled, almost invisibly most of the time, by the Amazon platform. The

---

3   AWS is a cloud-based platform, which can host and operate client websites. It takes advantage of the infrastructure used by Amazon – allowing search, payment, reviews and other ways of facilitating sales of products or services. The resulting web experience of customers seems proprietary, as if the company has a stand-alone website of its own making. But much of the interior architecture piggybacks on the software used to operate the main Amazon site. AWS is used to run a substantial number of websites that have no e-commerce component; the only thing Amazon is selling in those cases is software and cloud storage.

story of how Amazon went from being a bookstore to having sales that have been predicted to pass Walmart by 2022 is a story of understanding the importance of platforms.[4]

At the risk of pushing the analogy too far, Sears and Amazon both made 'homes' available on their platforms. Sears sold physical mail-order houses, with almost all the parts you would need to construct the physical building to live in. Amazon provides a 'home' on its servers for proprietary websites; the URLs of these businesses look for all intents and purposes as if they are owned by the company selling the products. But in fact all the server, and much of the software and protocols for clearing transactions, are running through AWS. In both cases, the ability to pay for an individualised private experience without having to pay for the costs of designing the home from scratch and creating the parts represents an enormous saving.

But Amazon is not really set up for sharing.[5] At this point, Amazon specialises in the 'deliver-to-own' model and it reduces the transaction costs of acquiring products

---

4   What is Amazon? *Zack's Notes*, 13 March 2019 (https://zackkanter.com/2019/03/13/what-is-amazon/).

5   Though one must be careful, since Amazon Studios actually do produce the company's own video content and the Prime distribution service allows seamless and nearly free 'rental' of that content. Prime Kindle likewise allows the rental of books. To the extent that the coronavirus pandemic advantages sharing, the very idea of owning may become obsolete. On the other hand, if sharing cannot guarantee safety from infection and so proves difficult to manage, the Amazon model may prove to be the sweet spot. Further, Amazon's 'cloud services' are nearly one-third of the total, twice as large as Microsoft's market share. This kind of 'sharing', where documents and resources are stored and edited in the cloud, represents another kind of sharing for which Amazon is obviously well situated.

that we are going to keep and store. But we are on the verge of a new kind of platform economy that is going to make renting, or sharing, a viable alternative to owning. Remember, Amazon used to sell books; we have forgotten about that, because now Amazon sells everything. Ten years from now, we are going to say, 'Uber used to rent a car and a driver, like a taxi company'. But Uber is arguably no more a taxi company than Amazon was a bookstore.

Uber can solve the problem of triangulation, transfer and trust for almost any product, except it is set up for the delivery and pickup of rental items. Uber could continue to deliver people, but the people could provide services. Maybe Uber will deliver food, as is already happening with Uber Eats. Maybe one day it will deliver power tools that I need for only a little while.

Of course, I don't know if these specific companies will survive. But the model of developing a platform using mobile smart devices, connected over a network of networks and running stand-alone modular software called 'apps', is likely to expand. It is easy to lose sight of that: the battle between Uber and the taxi companies is temporary, a distraction. The big battle is between something like Uber and something like Amazon, for platform primacy.

Selling trust raises the problem of antitrust

Of course, Amazon and Uber, or some other company that is just now being conceived, might all survive in this space. But there is a problem: platforms *want* to be big. Division of labour is limited by the extent of the market, but so is the ability to sell reductions in transaction costs. The problems of triangulation and transfer are both solved by scale: the more listings I have for products, the more both consumers and producers can take advantage of division of labour. Software that can clear 10,000 transactions a day can clear 1,000,000 transactions a day almost as cheaply, as long as the platform can expand storage and bandwidth. But the third transaction cost category – trust – is where the real economies of scale kick in. It is crucial to have an enormous portfolio of reviews, of information about agent reliability, to have lower-cost transactions. So 'trust' in the sense of assurance of performance creates potentially crippling problems of 'trust' in the sense of natural, scale-induced monopolisation of the market space. That is a problem we are just now trying to address.

To put it in more traditional terms, trust assurance exhibits network economies, because if everyone uses the same system then all the available information is shared. When I go on Amazon, I can find dozens of reviews for most products, and at least a few reviews for even the most obscure product I want to look at. If some other platform tries to enter this market, they have to solve the problem of outsourcing trust from scratch, building up an inventory of customer reviews. You can't do that until you have customers, but you can't win customers away from Amazon unless you have a critical mass of reviews, enough information to solve the problem of trust.

Economists and regulators think of this problem as an 'entry barrier'. An entrepreneur might come up with an idea for a new platform, a new way of selling access to services or stuff through reducing the costs of triangulation, transfer and trust. But at the outset the app that makes the platform accessible will have no portfolio of reviews for trust assurance. From the consumer's perspective, this raises the price of using the platform. In the case of some kinds of service, such as ride-sharing or apartment use, the cost of using the app without trust assurance in the start-up stages may be prohibitive: I do not care how cheap the service is if I worry about being robbed, raped or kidnapped.

Some of the same concerns, on a broader scale, are being directed at the monopoly features of social media sites such as Facebook, Instagram, Pinterest and Twitter. The reason they are so large is that we all want to have a shared platform for interaction. But that means that the usual threat of other firms entering the space, or consumers leaving the platform, is not credible. Competition doesn't have to be perfect to be effective, but it cannot be non-existent.[6] It is likely that public policymakers are going to have to rethink the traditional notions of antitrust and natural monopoly, because antitrust policies conflict with the economics of selling trust and convenience in this new market.

---

6 A particularly strident version of this argument is Zuboff (2019). Some of the problems the book identifies are overstated, but it is true that current ideas of antitrust based on monopoly pricing may miss the larger effects of 'bigness' in the market. Many of the firms Zuboff is concerned about offer their services free of charge, so the standard model based on deadweight loss of monopoly pricing is not useful.

Platforms don't sell stuff

That may come as a surprise to you, so let's make something clear: you think Amazon sells stuff. It does not. It licenses software. The way it came to this was almost accidental. In an interview with *Wired* magazine, CEO Jeff Bezos put it this way:

> Approximately nine years ago [in 2002] we were wasting a lot of time internally because, to do their jobs, our applications engineers had to have daily detailed conversations with our networking infrastructure engineers. Instead of having this fine-grained coordination about every detail, we wanted the data-center guys to give the apps guys a set of dependable tools, a reliable infrastructure that they could build products on top of.
>
> The problem was obvious. We didn't have that infrastructure. So we started building it for our own internal use. Then we realized, 'Whoa, everybody who wants to build web-scale applications is going to need this.' We figured with a little bit of extra work we could make it available to everybody. We're going to make it anyway – let's sell it.[7]

This is quite remarkable. It is true that Amazon originally thought of its business as selling stuff, first books and later a wide variety of other things. But Amazon quickly

---

7 Jeff Bezos owns the web in more ways than you think. *Wired*, 13 November 2011 (http://www.wired.com/2011/11/ff_bezos/).

realised that its real value was in bringing together buyers and sellers, providing a mechanism for clearing transactions reliably and safely, and providing information on sellers that outsourced trust to buyers. Amazon just needs to supply the software and the servers. People who wanted to sell, and people who wanted to buy, would self-organise into complex communities on the platform.

In fact, for many apparently proprietary websites, it is not obvious that Amazon is operating anything at all. AWS is able to morph into what look like bespoke firm websites, all the way reducing the transaction costs that would have prevented these companies from ever finding customers in the first place. Thus, Amazon is mostly a firm in the middleman economy, because it mostly sells reductions in transaction costs rather than sharing products. But Amazon is sharing AWS, because software always has excess capacity. All you have to do is copy it and adapt it to the particular needs of a new customer.[8]

To understand the middleman economy, one needs to recognise that the kind of disruption caused by Amazon is just the beginning. There is nothing special about the transportation of human bodies; the Uber software is a new and extremely dangerous (to other middlemen) way to sell reduced transaction costs. Uber is not a threat to taxi companies as much as it is a threat to Amazon. Instead of

---

8   In economic terms, software is non-rival in consumption: once the code is written, sharing it costs nothing more than the negligible expense of transferring and storing the code, and having some machine capable of executing that code. If it can be stored 'in the cloud', a service Amazon offers in 'Drive', then there may be no cost at all.

having to wait two days for your book, or your new alternator if you are working on your car, or a power drill if you are going to assemble an Ikea table, you will go to Uber, select the product you want to rent, and the Uber driver will deliver it, perhaps also taking a human passenger along the way. When you are finished you can have a different Uber driver pick up the mixer that you used to knead the bread, or the beautiful espresso machine you used after the dinner party last night. You don't have to drive, you don't have to handle money, and the rental fee is very small because the density of transactions spreads the cost of the rental item out over many renters.

Everyone has had the experience of making three trips to the hardware store to fix a tap, or a doorknob. And we all own things we would be happy to rent. The only reason we do those things is transaction costs. New software platforms that reduce the costs of triangulation, transfer and trust for one product or service can quickly be adapted to a variety of other products or services that none of us can foresee. What's important about the platform revolution is that the 'products' are the reductions in transaction costs that will commodify activities, services and unused resources in ways that until now have never been observed, nor even imagined.

Decentralised 'retail' ownership is too expensive

If people own things – clothes, tools, cars, houses – rather than rent the services that they provide, it is because owning secures services more reliably and at lower transaction costs than renting. But that could change. If I have a car, and a few minutes, and you need a ride, there is a mutually beneficial deal we could work out. But the transaction costs are expensive. The value in underused apartments – and cars, tools and a thousand other items – is at this point latent, literally locked up in the form of stuff.

As was discussed earlier, exclusive ownership of the underlying residual claims is essential for the system to function. But resting on that foundation is the possibility of 'sharing' durable goods over time, by making the right to ownership of use a modular and separable commodity (Kiesling 2016). This kind of sharing is not the normal way we think of that term; 'apportioning' or 'access' might be a better description. After all, no two people 'share' most Airbnb rentals; I get the flat for these two nights, you get it for the following two nights, and so on. As Eckhardt and Bardhi (2015) put it, calling these activities 'sharing' is actually misleading:

> This insight – that it is an access economy rather than a sharing economy – has important implications for how companies in this space compete. It implies that consumers are more interested in lower costs and convenience than they are in fostering social relationships with the company or other consumers. Companies that understand this will have a competitive advantage. For example, we are currently seeing the rise of Uber in the short-term car-ride market. Uber positions itself squarely around its pricing, reliability, and convenience. This is

encapsulated in their tagline, 'Better, faster and cheaper than a taxi.' In comparison, Lyft, which offers an almost identical service, positions itself as friendly ('We're your friend with a car'), and as a community ('Greet your driver with a fistbump'). Lyft has not seen nearly the same amount of growth as Uber, and a contributing reason is because they are putting too much emphasis on consumers' desire to 'share' with each other.

Still, modular commodification of this sort, with flexible and sometimes highly divisible units of time of use, does result in a kind of organised collaborative consumption. If I rent a Lime scooter, and then you rent a Lime scooter, and then someone else does, too, we are *sharing* that durable transportation device, all using it in on the same day and only for precisely as long – down to the second on the timestamp of the barcode scan – as we want to use it. The fact that we don't have to deal with each other is, as Eckhardt and Bardhi (2015) say, an advantage and not a drawback of this approach. I will use the word 'sharing' as a description of this sort of sequential temporal apportionment of access to use rights, with an underlying exclusive owner of residual claims, simply because that is how the word is often used now in the industry.

Even if you do own something, you can extract value from excess capacity by renting that thing out, provided we can solve the problems of triangulation, transfer and trust. Perhaps more importantly, even if you own almost nothing, you can still enjoy much of the value of ownership by renting from someone else.

Sharing or renting is enabled by a set of developments that have only come together in the past decade:

- Entrepreneurship applied to software reduces transaction costs more than automation reduces production costs,[9] for the same investment...
- Because of the availability of new software platforms...
- Operating on smart, portable hardware...
- Connected over internet or cellular networks.

Software programs in the sharing economy are both system (executing instructions) and application (storing, retrieving and interpreting information entered by users). Software 'apps' play the same role in reducing transaction costs that robots and automation have played in reducing production costs in the ownership economy. As I said above, to consumers, *all costs* are transaction costs. The traditional way to reduce costs is to automate to reduce labour costs, or otherwise cut money spent on production. The fertile new margin is using platforms to reduce transaction costs, reducing both actual prices and implicit costs, and expanding the set of things that we think of as commodities.

So far I have defined a platform as any institution, real or virtual, that reduces transaction costs along all three dimensions. But it is useful to define the larger concept that so far I have only alluded to. The platform economy as a whole can be defined as: *making more intensive and*

---

9   This process may be complicated by differences in the regulatory environment, of course. A recent summary of the 'software is inherently more profitable than hardware' view is Rambhia (2016).

efficient use of resources that are otherwise idle, with the consequent modification in the durable and average life of those resources as they are replaced.

Platforms can sell anything because they reduce the transaction costs of selling everything that passes across the platform. But 'sell' is perhaps too narrow a conception. Wikipedia is a platform. So is a tool library. Neither involves rental or even the payment of rent. Let me explain a bit.

Wikipedia and tool libraries: beyond rental

It may take a minute to understand why Wikipedia is a platform. But it is a useful example precisely because it is outside the usual rental-payment-for-use notion of market cooperation. There are many kinds of exchange that a platform can facilitate, and rentals are only one. On Wikipedia, the triangulation problem is that people sort themselves into groups based on their interest and knowledge. You can search for topics and subtopics that interest you or that you know a lot about, without having to know much about who anyone else is or what they do. You don't have to go out and find people, because Wikipedia has already divided and subdivided topics, and you can always suggest new ones if you want.

The transfer part, meaning that the thing to be shared is delivered and received and paid for, is unorthodox but it clearly works. You can edit almost anything on Wikipedia, if you have even minimal rights, which you can get by just signing up. Your edits are delivered just by saving. Of course, your 'service' is only delivered if it is accepted by the group that has authority over the page, which is other Wikipedia users. Someone else may edit your text, and an administrator or 'sysop' may delete all your changes and revert the page. But if you are serious and well-informed, your changes are likely to be welcomed, and incorporated.

The 'trust' aspect of Wikipedia is particularly interesting. The creation of the text is group-sourced, but members of the small communities who work on particular pages can identify each other, by their pseudonyms at least. If you are always just trolling or making malicious changes, your ability to suggest edits will be disabled. The group-sourcing of pages and subpages means that people are 'paid' with honour and esteem, respected as experts by others who are also experts, or perhaps just enthusiasts.

Wikipedia creates trust by the simple expedient of encoding a very low cost of exclusion of unwanted or incorrect material. If someone tries to manipulate an entry, or to introduce scatological or satirical content, it takes quite a bit of work to type and edit the 'new' entry. But the editors can, with only a few clicks, revert the entry to the last approved version. This asymmetry between the high cost of behaving badly and the very low cost of excluding those who behave badly is one of the chief innovations that have led to Wikipedia's success (Shirky 2009).

Wikipedia is remarkably consistent, even adept, in being able to provide the three things that a platform needs in order to have this service. But nobody is getting paid.[10] We only pay with honour in a sense of voluntarily contributing to the public good. This is true sharing, not renting. If a community can reduce the transaction costs of voluntary provision of public goods, new platforms such as Wikipedia may proliferate. And the idea that there must some kind of fee for service may start to disappear. There are ways of sharing that are based on honour and our consideration for other people – our desire to be lovely. Being part of a community that is expert on some subject that takes care of the Wikipedia entries on that subject means that a person has connections with somebody in South Korea, someone else in Europe, and so on. You have never met, but you are a community. This feeling of being part of something larger than ourselves is something that software platforms can advance.

An interesting recent example, one that is largely operating at a level below public recognition, but which is nonetheless quite widespread, is 'tool libraries'. It's not pure ownership, it's not renting, but it is cooperative sharing. And it doesn't appear at all in GDP, even though voluntary private associations like this dramatically increase our wealth.

Suppose there are thirty of us, all of whom live in a small neighbourhood, or even in a single block of a densely populated city. What we share is that each of us has a tool, a different tool, for woodworking or car repair, or some specialised activity we are all very interested in. Then the thirty

---

10 Actually, there is a thriving black market in creating Wikipedia pages. But the editors are vigilant about the practice, and examples are made of those who 'post for pay'. For background, see Pinsker (2015).

of us collectively have an extensive tool 'shop', though the shop doesn't exist in any one place. An organisation called Localtools.org provides software for groups of people to use to share tools, and to do it in a way that dramatically reduces the cost of having a well-stocked workshop. After all, good tools, especially specialised tools, are expensive, and it is the nature of highly specialised tools that most of us don't need them very often. But the right tool, exactly the right tool, is often indispensable for doing a task, or for doing it well.

A local group can form an ad hoc platform if members can solve the problems of finding each other, registering which tools are available (triangulation), making it possible to reserve one or several tools, effecting the delivery and return of the tool (transfer) and using sensors connected to software that measures abuse or damage to the tool, with a time stamp to attribute responsibility (trust). Each member of the group can have better tools than any of them could have afforded individually. This kind of organised sharing is enormously beneficial, because it also reduces storage costs dramatically. There are problems to be solved, but rapid progress is being made in solving sharing problems using ad hoc platforms on open source software.[11]

---

11 https://makezine.com/2012/05/29/how-to-start-a-tool-lending-library/

4   COMMODIFYING EXCESS CAPACITY

In my book, *Tomorrow 3.0*, I claimed that there are two different factors at work in the economic changes we see around us: selling reductions in transaction costs and commodifying excess capacity. Transaction costs are the expenses, including time, inconvenience and actual payments required to use the item. Excess capacity means the proportion of the time, or the capability, of the item that is underused or idle, combined with the opportunity cost or forgone alternatives for which the item could be used during that downtime.

In our kitchen, my wife and I have many drawers and cabinets. These storage spaces are filled with silverware, knives, a variety of cooking utensils, pots and pans, dishes and bowls, and a big heavy food-mixer with various attachments, including a pasta-roller and a sausage-grinder.

We use some of the cutlery (only a small percentage, because both of our sons have graduated from university and moved on to their own lives) once or twice a day, along with a few plates. We use a pot or two now and then, or a saucepan. The food-mixer sits there majestically, gathering dust. I have made sausage twice, in the past four years. (My wife finds sausage disgusting, and thinks that making it is even worse.)

The forks and spoons in the silverware drawer are used only rarely, and we have far more than we need for any time except when we are having a large dinner party, which happens at most twice a year. That means that, most of the time, there is significant excess capacity in our drawers.

But it's hard to imagine an app that could convert this excess capacity into a commodity, because the transaction costs are high compared with the cost of buying silverware and then owning and storing it. Not so for the food-mixer. It is expensive, rarely used, and the times when it will be used can be scheduled in advance. There are many apps that help people coordinate the use of appliances, but one of the most popular is peerby.com. Some of the apps involve rental fees, others are more like libraries. Regardless, these apps are platforms that commodify excess capacity by solving problems of triangulation, transfer and trust.

The sweet spot for the explosion of growth in the economy of *Tomorrow 3.0* is products that, and service providers who, have high excess capacity and value, but for which current arrangements of ownership and use produce high transaction costs. The reason that this is the sweet spot is that these items are not already thought of as commodities, but a clever and highly functional smartphone app can commoditise them taking advantage of the latent value just sitting around.

Unsurprisingly, two of the greatest successes in the new economy are high value, underutilised durable assets: cars and housing. We need to reconceive idle resources as being costly: a car in a parking space, or an empty flat in Carnaby Street during Fashion Week, is as much a waste of value as allowing crops to rot in the fields. The difference is that someone who already owns and uses a car or apartment most of the time needs only to cover the marginal, rather than average, cost to make sharing a paying proposition.

To see the difference, imagine that you are at university but are going home for the summer. You have a bicycle, which you can pay to store for three months, at £15 per month. You have already paid £200 for the bike, and you have that money tied up in it, but now you must pay another £45 to have it there in the autumn. Imagine that instead you could rent the bike out over the summer, for just £2 per month. You don't need to cover the average cost of the £200 value of the bike, you just need to cover the marginal cost of having it available when you return. Actually, you'd willingly rent it out for free, to avoid the £45 storage costs; the extra £6 rental revenue is pure profit.

Companies such as Spinlister are platforms that offer this kind of service. Obviously, they have to solve the problem of finding someone who needs a bike, who is willing to pay, who can pick up the bike, or have it delivered, and who won't damage the bike and will return it on time. The bike owner is ahead £51 at the end of the summer, 3 × £15 + 3 × £2, and someone got the use of a bike that would otherwise have been locked away.

Each of the first two great economic revolutions – the Neolithic and the Industrial – were the result of the attempt to develop new techniques for organising groups of humans and capturing the gains from cooperation. In the first revolution, the basis of the change was economies of scale in the technology of violence and gains from mutual cooperation organised as specialisation. In the second revolution, the Industrial Revolution, the motivation was profit, and so the dynamic force was (at least in large measure) entrepreneurship.

In both cases, the extent of the gains from specialisation was limited by the horizon of cooperation. After the Neolithic Revolution the development of cities meant that cooperation was much cheaper within the walls or the political boundaries of what defined the area protected (and held captive) by political power. After the Industrial Revolution the development of the technologies of production and exchange meant that the cooperation horizon was extended well beyond the city walls and the logic of market exchange drove the creation of institutions for reducing the transaction costs of trade between cities, moving across political boundaries.

Markets transform the cooperation horizon from city boundaries to the 'extent of the market', or the limits of the institutions of currency, transactions clearing and transport that human minds can create. Markets allow cooperation and foster mutual dependence over huge swathes of territory.

But in a dynamic sense, markets also feed back into the size of the cooperation horizon. Increased specialisation, especially in the form of the division of labour in Industrial Revolution production lines, pried open and integrated markets that had been closed and divided. Lower production costs 'wanted' to be global (and still do!); the result was a fundamental transformation in the way that people lived and depended upon each other. Instead of relying on local sources, buying shoes, saddles, knives and food from neighbours whose faces and names were known, people came to depend on impersonal markets. Why would anyone prefer an impersonal transaction to a personal one? If you ask them, they might say they don't. But the logic of division of labour drove costs down and elevated the quality and variety of goods so much that no other form of organisation was feasible.

This bears emphasising: the most dynamic actor in the play of market drama is the entrepreneur. In a static sense, we might think that entrepreneurs correct 'mistakes' in the allocation of resources. A mistake occurs when a resource – labour, time, human attention, or commodities – is used in some activity A, but its use value would have been greater in some other activity B. The superior alternative might be some other use now, or a use in the future, discounting for the rate of time preference.

In this view, everyone is an entrepreneur, and every day each of us corrects mistakes in the environment around us. If Abigail walks into a dark room and turns on the light, then the room's contents are rendered visible and so more valuable. If Abigail fails to turn on the light, and trips over the rubbish bin, that would be a mistake.

Of course, if Abigail turns on the light, she corrects a 'mistake', because now resources are more usefully employed. But she creates value only for herself. In this example, the problem is reduced to decision theory: Abigail has some resources – the room, the light switch – and some tasks to perform where increased light would be useful. The problem is to allocate existing resources or means among known purposes or ends. There is no social aspect to this problem: Robinson Crusoe, alone on his island, had resources, including his own labour and time. All an individual has to do is decide how to manipulate things to create more value for himself. Robinson Crusoe could, all by himself, discover and correct 'mistakes', by moving water and putting it on plants that will otherwise parch, and by using logs he has already cut to build a shelter from the sun and rain. Crusoe was creating value for himself. That is an interesting problem, but it is not entrepreneurship.

On a larger scale, entrepreneurs correct mistakes, because everything is in the wrong place, or rather it is not yet in the best place. They take these actions with the self-conscious intention to create value for others, because creating new consumer surplus is the source of profits.[1] Entrepreneurs engage in market activity, a fundamentally social activity involving the voluntary cooperation of other people, perhaps many other people.[2] In fact, the entrepreneur must create value first for those who supply his inputs and raw materials, paying more than input-owners value those inputs in their current uses. Then the entrepreneur must also create value for those who buy the products or services he creates, by selling for less than consumers

---

1   Consumer surplus is the benefit to consumers from buying a product, measured as the difference between what the consumer is willing to pay and the price at which the product is available in the market. Since this benefit is neither visible nor directly monetised, in the way that profits can be seen and measured, it is easy to underestimate the benefits to the economy of the innovations that produced the profits in the first place.

2   For the problem of whether an exchange is 'truly' voluntary, see Guzman and Munger (2019).

value the output. If the amount of revenues consumers willingly pay is enough to compensate the owners of inputs, and there is something left over to compensate the entrepreneur, then we know that net value has been created for the society.

Israel Kirzner gives a classic description of the relation between profit, value and entrepreneurship, in effect explaining why there are no £20 notes on the Battersea Park Circular. If prices for the same commodity differ widely, it is possible to make profits through arbitrage (Kirzner 1978):

> The multiplicity of prices represented opportunities for pure entrepreneurial profit; that such multiplicity existed, means that many market participants (those who sold at the lower prices and those who bought at the higher prices) simply overlooked these opportunities. Since these opportunities were left unexploited, not because of unavailable needed resources, but because they were simply not noticed, we understand that, as time passes, the lure of available pure profits can be counted upon to alert at least some market participants to the existence of these opportunities.

Kirzner defined entrepreneurship as 'awareness', the constant searching for profit opportunities. Entrepreneurs are constantly and energetically imagining alternative futures, new products and possible ways of organising production.

Imagination is a transient thought that transforms choice into the realm of the subjective, and the presence of transaction costs is a hindrance, a friction, on this mental act of transport.

As we discussed earlier, this distinction is central to the working of entrepreneurship. Steve Jobs did more than arbitrage price differences; he imagined new products. As Jobs put it, 'In the end, for something this complicated, it's really hard to design products by focus groups. A lot of times, people don't know what they want until you show it to them'.[3]

And Jobs was right, because he 'showed them' an iPod, a solid-state device that stored digital music and could reproduce it at high quality over small ear buds. The point is that entrepreneurs cannot rely on asking people what they want; entrepreneurs have to be able, in Shackle's words, to 'imagine' a different set of choices being offered (Shackle 1979).

Before the introduction of the iPod in 2001, the Sony Walkman was a popular (and profitable) device. People could move around or even exercise while listening to the radio or to cassette tapes. At one point the Walkman captured more than 50 per cent of the mobile music market. But then MP3 players came along, and the medium (tapes or compact discs) was divorced entirely from the message, in this case digital music. And even though people didn't know that MP3 was how they wanted to buy, store and carry their music, it turned out to be so. Steve Jobs and the Apple engineers imagined a different arrangement of productive resources. None of the resources needed to be

---

3 Steve Jobs: there's sanity returning. *Business Week*, 25 May 1998 (https://www.bloomberg.com/news/articles/1998-05-25/steve-jobs-theres-sanity-returning).

invented, and none of the digital processes for storing the music were especially difficult or innovative. But the package of features, the features that define the iPod and other products like it, was something new.

The problem is that the new technology wiped out the Walkman. Sony lost billions of dollars and was unable to offer a competitive product for several years. Sony laid off at least 10,000 workers and closed two large production facilities, causing at least 100,000 people to suffer significant economic harm. That makes entrepreneurship seem pretty destructive.

Remember, the harm was intentional: it was not an accident. Apple had specifically targeted the Walkman, the then-dominant product, as the consumer electronic device they wanted the iPod to displace.[4] It is easy to focus only on the apparent harm: the loss of Sony's stock value and the loss of all those jobs. But that is exactly what entrepreneurship and the associated disruption can cause. What this account misses is the benefit for millions of consumers.

Until now, entrepreneurship has generally taken the form of creating products, or new production processes, or new systems for transporting products that people want to buy. But the platform world will be different because entrepreneurs are turning their attention entirely to a function that until now has seemed boring. Many of the new entrepreneurs will be middlemen, enabling peer-to-peer exchange or some other form of cooperation.

---

4   The Walkman had sold more than 4 million units in the UK, and nearly 60 million worldwide (*Guardian* 2006).

5 MIDDLEMEN: SELLERS OF TRANSACTION COST REDUCTION

I have argued that entrepreneurs, at least when they are pursuing honest profits, and creating consumer surplus, are morally admirable. But what about middlemen, the people who buy products and then resell them at a higher price to someone else? We don't like middlemen, because they seem like parasites, buying products and then re-selling them at a higher price, but without improving the product along the way. If they make profits, surely they don't earn them. And in fact 'cut out the middleman' is a maxim of economy and prudence.

That criticism, though common, misunderstands what the middleman is actually selling. The middleman reduces transaction costs; that's actually all the middleman sells. Remember, a transaction can only take place if the offer from a potential buyer exceeds the marginal production costs of the seller plus transaction costs. That means middlemen enable transactions that otherwise could not take place. Transportation, information, assurance of quality through brand name, financial clearing services – all of these are means of making possible exchanges or agreements that otherwise would be blocked by transaction costs. Once you start to think in these terms, you realise that bankers, brokers, insurance sales representatives, department stores and the Sears catalogue are all examples of middlemen in one form or another. Far from being parasites, middlemen are essential for any complex market to function.

Consider a 'widget', a term economists use to represent a generic product. Imagine that Amelia owns a widget and would be willing to sell it for any price over £40. Cassie wants a widget and would pay any price less than £70. We can measure the value of the transaction to the consumer (Cassie) in this example: it is the difference between the amount that Cassie values the Widget (£70) and whatever price she actually has to pay. Of course, if the price is greater than £70, Cassie has the right to say no and to refuse the transaction. But any price lower than £70 creates a value to Cassie; the difference between the price agreed on and £70 is the 'consumer surplus'.

It is easy to miss the importance of consumer surplus as a driver of economic growth and disruptive change. Consider a question that might seem odd to you, when you first hear it: how much would you pay for an entrance ticket to a grocery store?

The reason that seems silly is that we all 'know' that you can enter grocery stores free of charge; it only costs you money if you buy something. There are exceptions, such as Costco, but then if you pay the £35 per year (at the time of writing, for a full membership), you can use the store free of charge. But why is that? Cinemas charge (a lot!) for popcorn and drinks, but they also charge an entry fee. Why don't grocery and home supply stores charge an entry fee?

One answer is: they do! Big box groceries require parking at a distance, a lot of walking around, and then standing in queues that are long, and also slow because people have lots of items in their trolleys. Convenience stores 'charge' a lower price, in terms of transaction costs: you can just run in and buy something quickly. There is usually just a short queue and the store is small. You can buy a couple of items, pay for them quickly, and walk the short distance back to your car. But the prices in convenience stores are much higher. That means less monetary consumer surplus on every item, but it may be worth it if you are in a hurry and want to conserve on transaction costs (parking, walking to and from the store, queueing, and so on). The convenience store is selling you a reduction in transaction costs (time, travel distance) in the form of higher prices. Convenience stores exist because people are willing to give up some of their monetary consumer surplus for lower transaction costs.

In the widget example, it seemed possible that there was a surplus available, because there are prices (say, £55) where Amelia would be better off selling and Cassie would be better off buying, compared with the situation if the transaction does not take place. To think of it another way, either Amelia or Cassie, or both, would be willing to pay something to be able to engage in the transaction. That's what 'surplus' means: new value is available because everyone is better off.

But Amelia may not know where or even who Cassie is, and it is expensive to go looking. Buyer and seller may be physically distant, meaning that there are transport costs.

And the medium of exchange may be cumbersome, requiring costs to clear the transaction if it takes place. These transaction costs may be £50 or more. Assume – just for convenience, it doesn't actually matter – that the transaction costs are split evenly. That means that Amelia will require a payment of at least £65 to sell the Widget and Cassie will pay at most £45. There is no price where the transaction can take place. And because of this Amelia and Cassie may not even imagine the exchange and make no effort to develop institutions for reducing the transaction cost. In standard economics we might call this a 'deadweight loss', but in fact this sort of problem is everywhere in an economy. The potential gains from 'correcting the error' of Amelia owning the widget instead of Cassie are unseen, even though Cassie values the widget £30 more than Amelia values it. It is important to note that transaction costs play the same role in economics that friction plays in physics: they are just dissipated and lost, like heat in an engine. But if the transaction costs are large, they can prevent the system from working at all.

We are missing the middleman, who sells reductions in transaction costs. Suppose that an entrepreneur, Coda, can devise a system that reduces transaction costs from £50 to £10, and can charge £5 to use this system. Then a transaction becomes possible, one that benefits all three participants, seller Amelia, buyer Cassie and the entrepreneur Coda. For example, suppose that Amelia charges £60 for the widget; £5 of the purchase price goes to Coda for managing the platform, and £10 is lost to transaction costs. But Amelia still ends up with £45 and she will accept any price over £40, so is better off by £5. The entrepreneur gets paid his £5, so he is better off. And Cassie gets a price of £60, when she would have paid £70, so she is also very happy with the result.

Is this just a theoretical example? Or could something like this work in the real world?

The middleman platform economy

Suppose you are walking through a neighbourhood in Knightsbridge on a weekend in August. Or December. If you look up, you'll see lots of dark windows. Apartments in very expensive neighbourhoods are sometimes empty for a week or more, meaning that people are paying £1,000 per week to store dishes and furniture. In fact, they are paying for locks, cameras and a doorman to make sure no one else uses any part of this space or this stuff.

But while these apartments are empty, the hotels are full and some visitors have to stay far out of the city, in Brent Cross or West Croydon. If the people who want a place to stay could just find someone who has a place, or a spare room, a mutually beneficial exchange could be arranged. But the transaction costs are prohibitive. It is hard to find a person you can trust, or even to find a person at all, who wants to pay rent for your apartment, or to find someone who has an apartment, or to arrange a price, or to arrange payment. Since the transaction costs are so high, no transactions take place.

Suppose you drive around the City, the financial district in London. If you stop at the corner of Wood Street and London Wall, you will notice there are several large parking garages within two blocks. They are full, too, most days, with thousands of cars sitting there doing nothing, but paying £3 per hour for the privilege. So, everyone is paying twice, first to own the car and then for land to store the car. They use the car for about 90 minutes a day, and otherwise store it in their home garage or on the street. All that space could be used for cycle lanes or parks or apartments, or something.

The reason to emphasise these two types of 'commodities' – housing and cars – is that they are in the sweet spot of high excess capacity and high (but reducible) transaction costs. The reader will recognise the 'sharing housing' example as the value proposition for Airbnb and the 'sharing transport' example as the value proposition for Uber or Lyft. These companies claim that they are not in (respectively) the hotel or the taxi business, but instead just operate software platforms that reduce the transaction costs of facilitating exchanges that were always possible, and always mutually beneficial, if the transaction costs problems could be solved.

The reason that Uber and Airbnb are such useful examples is that they blur the line between owning and renting. Why do we own things, rather than rent them? It may be that we enjoy ownership, or because we are concerned about our personal items such as combs or toothbrushes, of course. But as was discussed earlier, we are more interested in the services the durables provide, rather than owning the tools or the machines. I don't really want to own a car, I want convenient, safe and reliable transport services. I don't really want to own a house, I want a comfortable, anodyne and attractive space to spend the night, or maybe a week, or five years. Renting may be less expensive than owning, but many forms of transaction costs such as having to negotiate rent or repairs are reduced by owning.

To understand more concretely how transaction costs work, let us return to the example of Uber. It started as a taxi company (its name, at its 2009 start, was 'UberCab'), but it is clear that Uber is actually a software company, selling reductions in transaction costs. Some people have argued that the reason that Uber has succeeded is that it avoids the costs of complying with the regulations, taxes and restrictions that affect 'real' taxis. And that may be part of the story. But it is also true that Uber is a platform.

- **Triangulation**: You can call an Uber very quickly, and both your location and your destination are handled by the software: you do not have to communicate with the driver, except through the software. Triangulation can be much easier with Uber than if you have to call a taxi, get three calls from the driver who does not know the area and cannot find you. Uber takes someone with a car, and a few extra minutes, and matches that driver with someone who needs a ride.
- **Transfer**: The process of driving and paying is much easier with the Uber software. The driver does not need you to give directions, because you have already entered your destination, which the driver can then use to navigate while you think about something else.

Of course, you may want to take a route different from that suggested by the software, but the software 'sees' accidents and construction bottlenecks that you don't know about. Unless you have detailed local knowledge, the transfer process can be much better than the experience with a standard taxi company.[1] Finally, after the ride is over, the driver is paid, and tipped, without you having to touch your wallet.

- **Trust**: With a standard taxi, all you can see is a small, fuzzy photo of the driver and the taxi number (in London, all you can see is the driver's cab number; no name or photo is displayed, and complaints are not handled publicly). You are dependent on the hard work of faceless bureaucrats, people you can't contact and who are completely unaccountable to out-of-town guests, to make sure the driver is competent, and the taxi is safe. The record of such bureaucracies can be pretty dismal. With Uber, you can take advantage of hundreds of other 'pop-up' inspectors: other customers, people with accurate and up-to-date information, who leave ratings and who care about making sure other people don't have a bad experience. Further, you can see the name and registration number of the driver, without writing it down, because Uber stores it for

---

1 The use of 'The Knowledge' as a description of something required for taxi drivers is famous for London's 'black cabs'. The detailed mental map of the entire London area is a daunting entry barrier for a would-be hack driver. Except that the advent of GPS, especially combined with continuously updated information on traffic and accidents, can be nearly as useful as The Knowledge and is bundled free with the other services that Uber provides.

you. You know the company has the driver's personal and financial information. The system isn't perfect, but 'safer/less rude/more comfortable than a normal taxi' does not require perfection. Taxi companies, because of their complacency and highly regulated monopoly positions, are sometimes abusive to drivers and passengers alike, and have been remarkably resistant to improvements in customer service.

All three aspects of transaction costs – triangulation, transfer and trust – may be much improved by using the Uber software instead of a normal taxi: even if GPS is no better than The Knowledge, it saves aspiring drivers two years of staring at maps and driving around London for no reason.

And that is just the beginning: the combination of Uber software, universal 5G wireless service and powerful mobile smart phones can perform the same magic in a variety of other delivery and service transport arenas. Physicians can make house calls in rural areas; bearded hipsters can make artisanal pickles for delivery in Hoxton and Shoreditch; and grit-spreading trucks can be sent to the iciest roads in the remotest areas.

It is probably true that some of the value created by platforms such as Uber and Airbnb is the result of ducking costly regulations (as Howells (2020) has described). But there are two problems with this critique, as Howells acknowledges. Firstly, many of the regulations are anachronistic (because they were designed to solve problems of the 1970s) and overly restrictive (because they do more to protect producers than to allow consumers to enjoy new ways of doing business). The solution is to remove those restrictions from existing legacy businesses, not apply them to the new companies.

Secondly, avoiding regulation is not the real value proposition: the real value of the 'middleman economy' is the ability to make money by selling reductions in transaction costs. The best way to think of this is an analogy: software is to services as robots are to production industries. Once a platform is able to sell reductions in transaction costs, the original business model may be adapted to a variety of other activities that were unthinkable at the outset, and the existing service providers will find their world disrupted, perhaps forever.

Back to transaction costs: why ownership is too expensive

In the world of the new platform economy, entrepreneurs will compete by selling reductions in transaction costs, and much more intensive use will be made of existing resources. As the revolution proceeds, products will be constructed to be much more durable and more technically adaptable, but the number of *jobs* where people are employed making products will plummet.

This will be revolutionary and destructive. Until now, throughout the Neolithic and Industrial Revolutions, the value proposition has always been to make more stuff and sell the stuff. If you could make stuff cheaper, or better, or add something new to the stuff people want, you could make money.

I rent a large (10 × 20 square feet) storage unit and I pay nearly £120 per month for that space. In that storage unit, there is – among many other things – an almost-new outboard motor. No boat, just a motor. That motor is worth £1,000, which is quite a bit of money. But I spend more than that every year just to store it. Why? The answer is transaction costs. Or, to put it another way, organising exchange is expensive. If the exchange is expensive enough, it won't take place. In fact, if exchanges are expensive, we might not even consider a variety of items or services as 'commodities' in the first place. This seems obvious, but it isn't.

The father of 'transaction costs economics', Ronald Coase, began his life as an economist because he was puzzled. As was discussed in chapter 2, the question that puzzled him seems obvious, but once you start to think about it in the way Coase thought about it, it changes everything. In an interview, he put it like this (Coase 2002):

> We were discussing the way that businesses were controlled, and their plans were made, and all that sort of thing. On the other hand, [professors] told us all about the 'invisible hand', and how the pricing system worked itself, and you didn't need any plans and so forth. It seems quite natural to me now, though it doesn't seem to have bothered many other people: here you had these two systems operating simultaneously. One, within the firm, a little planned society, and on the other hand relations between firms conducted through the market. And yet, according to the way people looked at it, the whole thing could have been done through the market.

If markets and prices are so great, why are there firms? Notice that any theory that answered that question would have to answer a second related question: if firms are so great, why isn't there just one big firm?

In the case of markets, and firms in particular, Coase's answer is now standard in economics: firms will expand, or shrink, at the margin, until the cost of the last transaction organised internally equals the cost of using the external price system. In business schools this is presented as the 'make or buy' decision (Klein 2005) – the firm can acquire or build the capacity to make an additional input or service, or it can buy that thing in the open market. Changes in transaction costs will affect that boundary and the size of firms will change, perhaps quickly, as innovations in transaction costs management become available.

But the Coasian analysis applies equally well to a related question: why do people own things rather than rent? Again, the answer is transaction costs. But the particulars of the ways that transaction costs – triangulation, transfer and trust – are expensive tell us a lot about the problem.

If exchange is about stuff being in the wrong place, sharing is about there being 'more stuff than we need'. Instead of 'make or buy', the transaction cost problem of the future is 'rent or own'. Some people have called this 'the sharing economy', but that is misleading. Sharing would appear to imply communal use and even communal ownership. The platform economy will still involve private ownership, but each of us will own less, probably much less.

Why would this be true? The answer is transaction costs; consider the earlier example of the power drill. It is cheaper, even with the costs of having money tied up in the drill, and having to store the drill, to own rather than to rent – because renting is extremely inconvenient. The consumer wants access to a stream of services – services that can be cheaply and conveniently employed at the consumer's option – but the 'transaction' has until now been a purchase of the durable good because little is known about the future timing, duration or exact location of the consumer's desire to make holes in walls, or boards, or use the Phillips screwdriver head to assemble a table from Ikea or Homebase. What is missing from the discussion of the power drill and the choice to either rent or own, then, is the idea of time. A person may not want to have to accept the trouble and expense of owning tools, but that is the easiest way to ensure access to the services of that tool over time. To understand human choice about the form of ownership, it is necessary to understand the way people formulate plans and purposes, based on an understanding of time. Owning a durable item means that I am seeking to have access to the stream of services associated with that item over an indefinite future. The set of benefits and inconveniences and expenses associated with this choice are context dependent (Rizzo 1979).

Until now, in many cases consumers only owned the drill, or the car, because it is cheaper than 'sharing' through renting or some other cooperative arrangement. The new platform system provides a safe and convenient means of scheduling a window of rights to use the item, because entrepreneurs can sell reductions in the transaction costs of renting. The result will be that the quality and durability of the items being used (in effect, rented) will increase, but the quantity of items actually in circulation will plummet. This is still a system of private ownership, but now one owner will have residual control and enforcement rights to just a few extremely durable, industrial-quality items that are available to be rented, rather than many people owning low-quality and fragile items. The durability profile of items being used will change in response to the change in relative prices caused by the reductions in transaction costs. We will have far fewer tools, but each tool will be of much higher quality and durability.

The platform system is qualitatively different from the decentralised system of ownership and control we see now. Cairncross (1999) argued that the important innovation has been improved communications technologies and network economies in communications devices. But smart phones running apps and connected over the internet are just the *platforms* on which the actual cost reductions, and the rapid expansion of transaction density, depend. Consummating complex transactions without fear of fraud or robbery is more than an improvement in communications; it is a reduction in the cost and risk of sharing access to the use of durable items in ways that have never before been possible.

The same applies to the crowdsourcing of trust: it is not just information that is now being more cheaply transmitted. The software platforms of the future generate new information: impersonal, crowdsourced, trust-enforcing mechanisms, where before there was no reliable metric other than direct personal acquaintance. Crediting communications technology with embodying everything important about the transaction cost revolution is as misleading as crediting electricity for innovations in personal computing. The technology was necessary, but not sufficient without entrepreneurs who could realise the potential of that technology.

I have a policy that when I travel on business I never buy a car, but rent one instead. That is so obvious it sounds silly, but *why* is it obviously true? The answer is transaction costs. Suppose I fly into Manchester, and a friend and I intend to play golf at Worsley, and then Ellesmere. I could take taxis, or try to use the trains and buses, or I could buy a car.

Or I could rent a car from a particular kind of platform: British Rental Car. Often today that means that when I leave the aeroplane my phone immediately buzzes: software has sent me a text, with the exact location (say, Slot C18) of 'my' rental car. Of course, it is not really mine, because I am renting it. But that's the point: it is the car that I want, or rather the car I would want if I had to think about it.

I don't have to think about it, because my preferences for auto type, identification, insurance, fuel option, return date and payment are all already known by the software. All I have to do is walk directly to the car I want to rent, which has my name on the electronic screen above it and the keys waiting inside. The only actual person I see is the guard who checks IDs at the exit gate. All of the other aspects of the transaction are handled behind the scenes and (from my perspective) instantaneously, by software.

Different car rental companies offer competitive prices and similar cars. British Rental Car actually charges slightly more for each car per day, but the transaction costs of renting from British Rental Car are much lower. Consequently, the *total* costs of renting from British Rental Car are lower, and since to the consumer all costs are transaction costs, many people rent from them. British Rental Car makes greater profits and we renters get a lot more consumer surplus from the rental.

This all means that platforms make possible transactions that otherwise could not take place. Transport, information, assurance of quality through brand name, financial clearing services – all of these are means of making possible transactions that otherwise would be blocked by transaction costs. Companies that specialise in renting complicated commodities, such as cars, have worked out ways to reduce the transaction costs dramatically, both those faced by consumers and those faced by the company.

Most importantly, platforms can crowdsource trust. The software itself does not provide the information; what happens is that many people independently record their experiences and perceptions and what emerges is a powerful – and valuable – signal about reliability. I use one rental-car company rather than another because reviews tell me which one provides the best service; I don't have to rely on my own experience, but can free ride on the experience of others.

Older people seem to want systems of state regulation to solve problems of triangulation, transfer and trust. Younger people are used to relying on crowdsourcing, and are more comfortable with informal sharing and cooperation. If a young person is in a strange city, looking for a restaurant, the young adult doesn't ask the hotel concierge (who is likely to recommend a restaurant that bribed him) and they don't look at the local Food Standards Agency ratings. Young people use Yelp or some similar software program that sells reductions in transaction costs. Negative reviews are quite damaging, but informative. The system is not perfect, but it is quite good.

BlaBlaCar, the hitchhiking ride-share company (Munger 2018), and other systems such as Uber and Airbnb also rely on crowdsourcing trust. The stakes are much higher than choosing a restaurant, of course, but the system still works. Remember: the software records the identity and financial information of all parties, and provides a time-stamped record of all their interactions leading up to the actual transaction. It is certainly possible to fabricate an identity, but then it is possible to fake an employment record and work for a taxi company or hotel. Customers, whether they are drivers or passengers, know much more about their counterparts using BlaBlaCar than in the analogous situation of a shuttle or taxi driver.

6 RIDE-SHARING

There is another example of ride-sharing, one that is quite different from hiring a car from British Rental. It is the most widely known and most controversial, partly due to its labour practices and partly because it has been so aggressive about extending services into areas where it is not quite legal. Uber was discussed earlier, in terms of transaction costs: if I have a car and a few minutes, and you need a ride, we should be able to make a deal benefiting both of us. But we can't, because transaction costs are too high. Uber solves this problem, but not because Uber is a taxi company. Uber is a platform.

For a very long time, the answer to the question, 'How do I get there?', has been a specialised service provider, the hack or taxi. The problem of needing a ride is generic and ancient. But hackney carriages, as London taxis are technically called, are relatively expensive. In many cities in Europe and the US, taxis can be difficult to find or contract with, and drivers sometimes have dirty cars, are abusive and drive aggressively. Even in London, where the black cabs are a revered tradition, there have been complaints. As Harry Mount puts it:[1]

---

1   The case against London cabbies: it's time to end the archaic privileges of taxi drivers. *The Spectator*, 1 February 2014 (https://www.spectator.co.uk/2014/02/the-case-against-london-black-cabs/).

With their exclusive rights protected by the Public Carriage Office, and their rivals held back, black cabs behave like any cartel – they squeeze their advantages for all their worth. On countless occasions, I've gone nuts at the little tricks drivers use to extend the journey time: gradually slowing down in approach to a green light, willing it to turn red; slowing down before a zebra crossing in the hope that a pedestrian will come along; moving off at the lights at a glacial pace; piling on infinitesimal fractions of seconds to the journey by taking a particularly wide arc into a corner; scrupulously staying out of yellow boxes painted over crossroads, apparently for Highway Code reasons, but really to catch another red light.

To be fair, many drivers can tell analogous stories of nightmarish passengers, terrible traffic, and four-hour waits at Heathrow for a £8.70 fare. The point is that there was very little that passengers, or drivers, could do if things were just normally bad. Passengers couldn't give drivers a bad review and drivers couldn't give abusive or drunken passengers bad reviews.

But even putting aside problems with obnoxious or unscrupulous drivers, it can be difficult to find a taxi in cities such as London, New York or Paris. Once, after waiting at a taxi stand for 40 minutes in Paris, we decided just to take the Metro, even though it meant walking half a mile in the rain at both ends of the trip. That beats having to wait an indeterminate time in the rain.

That's really the story of Uber. It was not so much a business plan as a response to the fact that traditional taxi services were plagued by problems.

Uber: the origin

Like many origin stories, Uber's birth has taken on an air of myth. But the origin derives from the restrictions – legal and practical – on availability and the cost of employing drivers full time, which made taxis in the San Francisco and Silicon Valley area both expensive and inconvenient. Taxis are too expensive and you can never find one when you need one.

One version of Uber's creation story is given by co-founder (and later CEO) Travis Kalanick.[2] He claims that he and Garrett Camp (original investor and co-founder), while attending a 'Le Web' conference in snowy Paris in 2008, stayed up most of the night (as they often did, having fairly recently sold their own web start-ups, StumbleUpon for Camp and Red Swoosh for Kalanick) 'jamming' on ideas for a new venture. They kept coming back to how terrible taxis were as a way of getting around, particularly in San Francisco. According to Kalanick, 'getting stranded on the streets of San Francisco is familiar territory' for those who live there.

The original idea (remember, these men were both busy and wealthy) was using an app to share limos, selling (while also using) pieces of the costs of a driver, a £100,000 Mercedes S-class and a parking spot in a nearby garage. They laughed at the idea that they could write an iPhone app that would sell pieces of this service on demand, when-ever the driver was on duty.

---

2   Uber's founding. Uber newsroom, 22 December 2010 (https://newsroom .uber.com/ubers-founding/).

Of course, they quickly identified that the entrepreneurial opportunity was not in buying the car–driver–garage combination and selling pieces of it. The big innovation was the software platform that would allow others to rent and to use cars they already owned. Nonetheless, they expected that the business would be 'low-tech, mostly operational'. They tested the concept in New York City in January 2010 around SOHO/Union Square and worked on making the system efficient and less buggy. The model they were trying to subvert used fixed pricing, physical maps, line-of-sight hailing, company-owned cars and analogue phones. The switch – to a software-operated, GPS-based, automatic charge processing and dynamic algorithmically driven pricing system with 'volunteer' drivers supplying their own cars – required a massive conceptual reinventing.

The team (with Camp taking a smaller role, but first employee Ryan Graves recruited to replace him) launched the full commercial version in San Francisco that 2010 summer. By the end of that year, hundreds of drivers had signed up and more than ten thousand passengers had paid for rides. In 2011 Uber expanded to several other US cities and in 2012 began to operate abroad, beginning with France and the UK.

In 2013, Uber started offering services in South Africa and India; in 2014 international expansion took a more aggressive turn, adding China, Nigeria and other countries. By March 2020 Uber was operating in more than 70 countries worldwide, with more than 14 million rides each day. The total number of drivers is hard to estimate, since many people drive for Uber part time, particularly in the

US, where regulations in many cities are more lax. But it is safe to say that there are a million Uber drivers in the US, with forty thousand drivers in the UK, and nearly four million worldwide.

Not a taxi company?

The important thing, in terms of its significance as a platform, is that Uber is not a taxi company. It turned out that the software that Uber is based on was first used to reduce the transaction costs of triangulation, transfer and trust in local transport, but there is no reason to expect that function to be primary for long. There are many other kinds of goods and services for which the particular combination of location, connection, payment and reputation that Uber provides will prove valuable.

In summary, Uber is a software platform. Uber the corporation sells reductions in transaction costs, enabling a wide variety of transactions that otherwise would not take place and commodifying excess capacity. Until now, we have never even noticed the transactions that do not take place, because it's hard to imagine a world where people can make money by selling reductions in transaction costs.

That's the world of platforms. The specific nature of the 'service' can be surprising, and very detailed. Suppose you have to be out of town for three days, and you are thinking of putting your dog in a kennel, something that costs you money and your dog hates. What if someone wanted to have a dog for just a few days? That's BarkNBorrow (sorry, pup-lovers: only in the US at this point!). There are lots of people who would like to have a dog to play with for a weekend, and your dog gets nice walks instead of being locked in a cage.

Of course, the transaction cost problems with these activities would once have prevented Uber-like matching services such as Spinlister (from chapter 4) or BarkN-Borrow. How would you find each other (triangulation)? How would you get together, negotiate a price and make the payment, and hand over whatever it is (transfer)? How would you know that the person is going to take good care of your bike or your dog (trust)? The answer, as always, is that smart people may be able to work out ways to sell reductions in those transaction costs. Uber is not a taxi company, Spinlister doesn't sell bikes and BarkNBorrow doesn't rent dogs. They sell reductions in transaction costs so that mutually beneficial forms of cooperation that were always latent can become real.

Surge pricing

One objection many people have made to Uber, and other platform economy companies, involves their dynamic pricing practices. Several incidents have enraged voters and attracted the attention of regulators. Perhaps the most famous was the aftermath of a terrorist attack in Sydney in December 2014.

Uber's fares are generated by an algorithm that looks at location, the number of riders hailing cars, and the number of cars in the area (though not the distance between the car and the potential passenger). The algorithm does two things: firstly it 'rations' access to rides; if there are more riders than rides, some system is necessary for deciding who gets picked up. Secondly, the algorithm raises fares received by drivers in a way that attracts more drivers. This counterbalances, at least in part, the rationing problem by making more rides available at times of peak demand.

Note the elegant simplicity of the price signal: drivers don't need to know why there is high demand, or what conditions are leading to a shortage of cars in an area. All they need to know is that if they drive to that location and pick up passengers they will be paid a premium.

What had happened in Sydney was clearly bad. A terrorist had taken 13 people hostage, and thousands of people in the city centre were desperate to get away. There were not nearly enough taxis and buses for everyone to leave at once; the bridges leading out of the centre were clogged. Thousands were stranded. The only cars and vans heading downtown across the bridges towards possible danger were ride-share drivers. When they learnt there were high fares to be earned, they left their apartments, got in their cars and drove to where people needed rides.

Let's consider two hypothetical people. Zander is an Uber driver who hears of the higher price and drives into potential danger to provide a ride to a desperate person who wants to get out. Ysidro is Zander's next door neighbour, watching the hostage crisis unfold on television. Ysidro feels great sympathy for the people in the city centre and stays glued to the television all afternoon. Who is more morally admirable?

Strangely – and this is very strange when you think about it – most people think Ysidro, who does nothing but has feelings of sympathy, is more moral than Zander, who actually gets in his car and drives into danger to provide a service people actually need. Uber was castigated for using price as a means of getting help to people who needed it. One user, Matthew Leung, said 'I have never, ever seen it at four-times [the normal rate] and I'm a 1% top Uber user ... I understand the way the business works – higher the demand, higher the charge – but four-times at $100 minimum is ridiculous. Almost price gouging at its worst'.[3]

The accusation does sound pretty bad: Uber raised prices, taking advantage of the desperate need of people to find rides fast. But that is not what really happened. The price went up simply because there was a spike in demand for rides in a particular area of the city. All that the algorithm knew was that suddenly, in the middle of an afternoon, thousands of people all tried to take Uber rides at once. The algorithm tried to match passengers with rides and to attract more drivers to the area quickly; the only way to do that is to raise prices.

And the algorithm worked in just the way it was supposed to. It is useful for me to learn whether someone else values a thing or a service more than I do. If the price were artificially suppressed, then someone in the suburbs who could walk or take a bus might take the Uber ride that is

---

3   Uber charges premium rate for rescue from Sydney siege. ITP.net, 15 December 2014 (https://www.itp.net/601302-uber-charges-premium-rate-for -rescue-from-)

desperately needed by someone else, in a different part of the city. Without price signals, we don't know the value of resources. And the higher price attracted more drivers, people like Zander who were not watching TV but who were looking at their phones and noticed the higher price. This was not price gouging at all, because the price was responding straightforwardly to needs and the shortage of resources; no human being jacked up prices after hearing about the crisis.

But there is a more important question: what is the alternative? The answer is that surge pricing is always with us; it is unavoidable. If a service is scarce, it must be rationed. The two ways of rationing, at least in private markets, are bidding up the monetary cost, or queuing, which bids up the cost of waiting for a ride. From the perspective of the consumer, the total 'price' is the sum of the monetary cost and the value of the time spent waiting to be picked up. That means that there is a difference between the cost to the consumer and the value received by the seller. It is useful to consider that difference in more detail.

- *Total cost to the consumer* includes search costs, transportation to a 'market' or place where the product is available, waiting in line to obtain or pay for the product, dealing with transportation of the product itself to where it will be used, opening and then disposing of the packaging, working out the instructions about how to operate the product, and dealing with the probability that the product doesn't work as expected or breaks.

- *Total value received* by the producer includes the money, or at a minimum some highly liquid equivalent, as a result of the sale.

This difference is generic, applying to almost any economic transaction. By monetising the deadweight loss of queuing, platforms capture much of the value now being wasted by the friction of transaction costs. A simple example illustrates the problem. Suppose a person, Alice, wants to rent a kitchen appliance. Alice will pay up to a total of £15 to rent the appliance. Boris owns the appliance, and would be pleased to rent the appliance for any amount over £5. Normally, the economist would draw a £10 'bargaining space', representing the surplus to be divided.

But this is nonsense. Alice has to find Boris, they have to agree on a price, and some assurance of compensation to Alice for injury using the product or Boris for loss if the product is damaged must be arranged; the appliance must be obtained and transported and then returned. All of these things are likely to result in some queuing, which imposes a cost on Alice that is not received by Boris but which is simply wasted in the system.

As previously mentioned, transaction costs play the same role in markets that friction plays in physical systems; just as friction reduces the power of a motor and is burned off as heat, transaction costs reduce the value of an exchange and are dissipated as deadweight loss.

Imagine that the total transaction costs of information and inconvenience amount to £12; since Boris must receive £5, the 'price' perceived by Alice is £12 + £5 or £17.

There is no bargaining space, since the cost to Alice is £17 and the most she will pay is £15. That is, we have monetised the value Alice would be willing to pay to avoid the transaction costs, providing her with the information she needs and increasing the convenience of the process so she doesn't have to drive around or queue.

There is no bargaining space; there will be no transaction. And Boris could work hard to reduce the cost of the appliance rental, from £5 to £4, and yet there would still be no effective demand for it. But notice it should be possible to sell the reduction in transaction costs, alongside the sale of the product itself. Either Boris or Alice, or both, would be willing to pay something to have access to a platform that reduces transaction costs from £12 to £3. Let us suppose the app/platform owner charges £2 per transaction.

Now it is clear that Alice and Boris could agree, firstly, to split the £2 licensing fee to use the platform and, secondly, to split the resulting bargaining surplus, if there is one. The platform does not reduce transaction costs to zero, of course; let us say transaction costs are still £2, £1 of which is absorbed by each party. In that case, Alice will pay £15, Boris will accept £5. The gross surplus must be reduced by £2 transaction costs, leaving £8 net surplus. Each party must pay £1 – half the licensing fee – leaving £6 net surplus. They agree on a price of £10, and each is better off by £3 as a result of engaging in the exchange.

It is easy to restate this kind of example in terms of the ride-provider and the passenger for Uber. From the perspective of the producer (in this case a taxi driver), the costs include the rental of the car, the 'rental' of the

Uber-authorisation, the value of the time spent in the taxi, the costs of insurance, and so on. From the perspective of the consumer (the potential rider), the costs include all of the producer costs (because the driver will only be there if he is making a profit). But the final price also includes the costs and inconvenience of waiting.

If you have trouble finding a taxi, the dispatcher or driver has trouble finding you, or you have to wait (as is common) 45 minutes or more for a ride, these are real costs, even though each is 'just a transaction cost'. To simplify, then, the cost to the passenger is the sum of the fare and the waiting time plus the risks of the ride and the inconvenience of having to pay (often in cash) and negotiate a tip with a potentially angry and aggressive driver. Uber and other ride-share companies eliminate some of these transaction costs.

Of course, many of us have had the experience of calling an Uber, only to see that there is a 'surge' (temporary period of elevated price due to high local demand) or a long wait time (because there are no cars nearby). It is tempting then to go to another ride-share app, such as Wheely or Gett. But to find out if those are cheaper, or can pick you up faster, you have to get out of the Uber app and start another app.

This kind of thing was a problem twenty years ago, when airlines and hotels started offering websites so people could search for reservations and prices. A number of companies recognised that it was possible to go 'meta', offering reductions in transaction costs to access the sites that themselves were offering reductions in transaction costs. Websites such as Orbitz, Expedia and others could collect and curate all the information for all the flights or hotels that offered the service you were looking for.

Unsurprisingly, entrepreneurs have recognised and acted on the same opportunity for ride-sharing. Companies such as RideGuru or Gett give you one-screen information about price and wait-time for a pick-up. If one company has a surge and another a long waiting time, a person in a hurry may pay the higher price, while someone on a looser schedule may wait for the cheaper car. This all seems complicated (you contact RideGuru to contact Uber to contact a local driver), but it operates instantly and nearly invisibly.

Another way to think of this is that a licensing system, by restricting entry into the taxi service industry, uses an uncompromising but effective form of surge pricing:

Consumer price = meter price + waiting time + search costs

In times of high demand, the person wanting a ride has to make repeated phone calls to the dispatcher, or stand in the rain waving at already full taxis, sometimes getting into shoving matches. The interesting thing is that the price (paid by consumers) rises to clear the market, but in the case of licence-restricted taxis with fixed meter rates there is no surge in the prices received by producers. That means that all of the 'surge' in price (including waiting time and inconvenience) falls on consumers, but is not received by producers.

Suppose you had a more flexible surge system for adjusting price. In particular, suppose that potential ride producers could respond to high prices quickly by leaving their apartments and starting to provide rides in high demand periods. The system could be described this way:

Producer price (meter rate) + waiting time (consumer cost) = flexible producer price (surge rate)

That is, suppose that there was some way to increase the number of producers, at high demand times, by increasing the meter rate. It is true that consumers would pay higher prices in terms of fares, but the value of time lost waiting would fall exactly in proportion to the increased price.

Most people have never thought this through, but it is just basic economics. Consumers pay the same amount, regardless of whether surge pricing is allowed, because if surge pricing is not allowed, consumers pay much higher transaction costs in terms of searching and waiting. We have surge pricing now and we've always had it. Just ask someone who has tried to get a taxi in London or Paris at 7.30 p.m. on a rainy Saturday night: you can pay with money, or you can pay with time, but surge pricing still happens.

So, there is the real answer to the question I posed earlier. Uber exists because innovators worked out a way to sell reductions in transaction costs. And the 'surge pricing' problem is not really a problem at all, but a solution. If surge pricing involving the payment of higher fares is outlawed, the only alternative is to pay 'surge' prices by queuing, which means not being sure when you'll get a ride, and searching for a ride by standing on a busy street in rain and waving your arms like an idiot. Those are costs, too, and in a time of shortage those costs increase to match the number of passengers and the number of rides in traditional taxis.[4]

Maybe you think that is okay. But surge pricing based on money actually increases the supply of the service at just the time when people need it. The problem with surge pricing based on varying transaction costs is that it provides no incentive to offer more of the service.

Uber doesn't just deliver people, which is what cabs do; in fact, Uber is quickly becoming a platform that delivers all sorts of products and services *to* humans. It is a software platform that sells reductions in transaction costs. There is no reason that it only needs to deliver humans to locations. More and more, Uber and other services that are 'Uber, but for –' will be delivering all sorts of things to humans. Like Amazon, the real value proposition for Uber will be opening the platform to permissionless innovation, to uses that the platform's creators had never intended or foreseen. The short-run forecast is disruption, but as

---

4   Interestingly, there is some evidence that the entry of ride-sharing services actually increases the quality of traditional taxi services. Scott Wallsten looked at the frequency, severity and types of complaints about behaviour of traditional taxi drivers in several cities, including New York and Chicago. See: Has Uber forced taxi drivers to step up their game? *The Atlantic*, 9 July 2015 (https://www.theatlantic.com/business/archive/2015/07/uber-taxi-drivers-complaints-chicago-newyork/397931/). There are many factors at work, but it appears that taxi drivers were motivated by the competition from ride-share platforms to 'step up their game', driving less aggressively and being more responsive to consumers' desires on route and behaviour. For a more general analysis of racial and gender treatment, see Ge et al. (2016).

Boettke and Candela (2017) have pointed out, over the longer term such platform innovations are likely to foster a 'virtuous cycle', the implications of which are impossible to foresee.

7 PROBLEMS WITH DISRUPTIVE TECHNOLOGY

There are two problems with Uber or anything 'Uber-like'. One is fairness and another is economic disruption. It is easy to conflate them, because people usually try to use justice to defend their self-interest. But let's keep them separate. I will take up the fairness argument later in the chapter; for now let's focus on disruption.

Uber is a disruptive technology. Existing forms of economic organisation resist disruption, sometimes fiercely, and quite rationally in terms of their own self-interest. What economists call 'disruption', after all, is hundreds of people losing their jobs forever, because the jobs no longer exist in anything like the same form.

When cars were being introduced, the people who made buggies and took care of horses reacted by trying to pass regulations that made cars impossible, or at least so inconvenient that the cars would be blocked and their use would be curtailed and restricted. In 1896, the Pennsylvania General Assembly passed (with not one dissenting vote) a so-called 'red flag' law, based on a UK ordinance (Karolevitz 1968). That name comes from the requirement, found in many cities in the US and England, that any self-propelled vehicle be proceeded by a man on foot walking (yes, walking) 50 to 100 feet in advance, waving a red flag in warning. Sometimes, a noise maker – a whistle, or drum – was also required, though presumably the sound of a steam or internal combustion engine was, given those primitive levels of development, quite enough warning on its own.

Here is a summary of the Bill, which was passed by the Pennsylvania legislature but vetoed by the governor (Karelovitz 1968: 192):

> [A car that] upon chance encounters with cattle or live-stock to (1) immediately stop the vehicle, (2) immediately and as rapidly as possible disassemble the automobile, and (3) conceal the various components out of sight behind nearby bushes until equestrian or livestock is sufficiently pacified.

Why would such a silly law be passed? Legislators may have had legitimate concerns about safety, since the new technology seemed dangerous. But much of the problem with the new technology was that it would threaten the settled way of life for thousands of people. In 1900 there were nearly 27 million horses and mules in the US (and only 100 million people); in the UK, the analogous figures were 3 million horses for 40 million people. By 1970 horses had largely disappeared from the lives of the Americans and British, except for some rural areas and the paddocks of the wealthy.

The skills and resources required to train, feed, house, ride and otherwise make use of horses were very valuable. But these skills quickly became almost worthless, in economic terms. One trope of economic disruption dates from these wrenching changes in moving from horses to automobiles: people with obsolete skills are compared to 'buggy whip makers'.

Economic evolution works by replacing existing products, services and ways of delivering them with new or cheaper ones. Schumpeter called this process 'creative destruction', but we tend to value the 'creative' part and underestimate the 'destruction' part. Economic competition implies the replacement of inferior systems of production and distribution by more efficient mechanisms. Better ideas work through killing off the old ways, the old firms and the old jobs. It's brutal. Instead of 'survival' in a biological sense, the competition takes the form of trying to earn a profit by providing higher-quality goods and services at lower costs. A company that fails to earn a profit and continues to lose money effectively 'starves' at some point and goes out of business. Consumers win, in this system, but it is tough on employees. In the US, at least 5 million people – saddle and tack makers, trainers, stable owners, manufacturers of buggies and coaches, and so on – lost their jobs when horses were largely replaced by gasoline-powered cars, trucks, trains and ships.

Why so much destruction? It is tempting to blame management, because 'buggy whip makers' failed to foresee the changes in their industry. That would have required quite a bit of foresight, of course. In fact, Henry Ford is said to have pointed out that consumers themselves cannot foresee fundamental changes, even though consumers drive the changes: 'If I had asked consumers what they wanted, they would have said 'Faster horses!'". If consumers can't foresee change, how can the businesses that serve consumers forecast change?

Sabotage: when the referee is also a player

When it comes to a battle among technologies and products for the affection of consumers, we tend to think of the state as a judge, a kind of umpire. But sometimes the umpire plays favourites. In June 2015, the California Labor Commission ruled Uber drivers must be legally reclassified from private contractors to employees.[1] Given California's requirements for pay, healthcare benefits and hours for employees, this was a significant blow to Uber's operation in the Golden State. The decision was extended by the California Supreme Court in a case involving Dynamex, a shipping company. The court decided that California would conform to the so-called 'ABC test', a three-pronged determination if a company's workers were employers or private contractors.

An employer must meet three requirements to prove their workers are independent contractors. Under the terms of the Dynamex decision, these are:

- Does the contractor provide the service free from the company's control?

---

1 Defining 'employee' in the gig economy. *New York Times*, 18 July 2015 (http://www.nytimes.com/2015/07/19/opinion/sunday/defining-employee -in-the-gig-economy.html).

- Is the service provided outside the company's core business (e.g. a janitor working at a law firm)?
- Is the employee an independent professional engaged in providing their service to companies other than just the one in question?

My claim is that we have to take a step back. At present, taxi companies fail to understand what business they are in. They think they sell transport, but they actually sell reductions in transaction costs so people with a car can find someone who needs a ride, and then the app makes that possible. The idea is that some consumers do not want to own a car; they do not even want to rent a car. Consumers want to be somewhere different from where they are now and they want to do it in a way that is fast, convenient and financially invisible. It is true that taxi companies, in addition to providing the service of matching drivers and riders, may also own the cars themselves. But that is not a necessary component of this business.

Further, if you have ever had trouble paying a driver or finding exact change when the driver is reluctant to take a credit card, it is easy to forget how important the 'invisible' part is. When I was working at the Australian National University in Canberra a few years ago, I happened to be invited to a dinner party outside the city. And I was asked to make sure that two other visitors, a philosopher visiting from Poland and his wife, also made it to the dinner. I called an Uber and the three of us headed off.

I could see the elderly Polish gentleman craning his neck, looking for a meter. He was a veteran traveller and

I'm sure he had had the experience of using sketchy 'street taxis' in areas such as Latin America where kidnapping was a real possibility. Then, when we got to the destination, I unthinkingly just thanked the driver and got out. My elderly ward and his wife started talking to each other angrily in Polish and then the old gentleman took out his wallet and tried to pay the driver. They had never used Uber before and had no idea that the pricing, directions and payment were handled seamlessly and invisibly by the Uber software.

Taxis sometimes do a pretty bad job of all three of those things. The price has to do with distance travelled, so taxis often take unsuspecting passengers out of their way. Directions may be difficult and often result in long discussions and confusion, particularly in other languages. And paying can be difficult and even dangerous, because you have to carry cash and the driver has to carry a lot of cash, or you have to give the driver your credit card in a way that makes it easy to steal the information. None of these things are problems with Uber, Wheely or ride-share apps in general, and that's why those platforms have been so successful. The providers of ride-share services are the part-time drivers who own cars and pay all the fixed costs already.

Uber itself is not a transport company; it is just a platform for connecting a willing buyer and a competent, nearby seller who has some extra time. Uber cannot be an employer of drivers, because it is not a seller of transport services. Uber does have employees, of course, but they are the people working on code, security and websites to help connect users. If you think that Uber is a transport company, you are one of Levitt's 'buggy whip makers', someone who does not understand what the real value proposition is (Levitt 1960).

The California 'court' (which is not a court at all but the Labor Commission) said this, in response to the suit by disgruntled driver Cassie Berwick:

> Defendants hold themselves out as nothing more than a neutral technological platform, designed simply to enable drivers and passengers to transact the business of transportation. The reality, however, is that Defendants are involved in every aspect of the operation.

But, no. That would be something like claiming that Open-Table is a restaurant company. What OpenTable[2] does is to provide information about a transaction (make a reservation at restaurant X, at restaurant Y, or stay home) that will take place only if the consumer decides she wants to eat at one of those restaurants, which are not owned by OpenTable at all. Yes, OpenTable is involved in the restaurant business, pretty deeply. But what they are selling is information.

Of course, it really is true that with Uber (unlike with OpenTable) you pay the company and they pay the driver. But the rates are fixed and known in advance (yes, even during a surge). Uber just acts to clear the transaction conveniently and quickly, so you don't have to carry cash and

---

2   https://www.opentable.co.uk/

neither does the driver. It is just not true that Uber is pay-ing the driver. The passenger is paying the driver, in a way that is more convenient for everyone. Uber just handles the transaction.

Why did the government, supposedly the referee, decide to become a player in the game?[3] From the perspective of the state, the people who work in traditional transport ser-vices are decent, hard-working, salt-of-the-earth people who are just trying to make a living and, in many cases, support their families. Shouldn't they be protected? The harm done by creative destruction is real. In fact, in 2010 there were more than a quarter of a million workers in Bu-reau of Labor Statistics job category 53-3041, 'Taxi Drivers and Chauffeurs'.[4] By May 2015 that number had fallen to 180,000, and there is every reason to expect it will continue to fall. Every one of those workers is someone who is trying to make a living, and most of them are trying to play by the rules.

The problem is that 'the rules' do not allow for adap-tation to changing circumstances. Levitt (1960) blamed management for being unable to understand 'what is your real business?', but regulators make the problem even worse. By definition, it is hard to regulate an industry that does not exist. And if political decisions are based on votes, it will always be true that there are more existing jobs

---

3   For an overview of problems of 'government failure', see Keech and Munger (2015).

4   Employment and unemployment among youth – summer 2014. *Bureau of Labor Statistics.* USDL-14-1498, 13 August 2014 (http://www.bls.gov/news .release/youth.nr0.htm).

depending on obsolete technology than there are votes from workers whose jobs have yet to be created.

The reason that traditional employee-driven (pardon the pun) transport services are disappearing is that software is cheaper, faster and better than employees, from the perspective of consumers. Taken as a whole, the costs to consumers of paying more, ranging from monetary costs to transaction costs of various kinds, is far higher than the benefit to employees of keeping their jobs. But the costs to consumers of preserving the 'buggy whip' version of transport is dispersed, and it may be invisible because much of the cost takes the form of transactions that do not take place.

The real solution is for the umpire – in this case, the state – to quit playing the game and go back to a neutral role. Of course it is tough to see one side get crushed, especially when those workers are willing to contribute almost any amount of money and time to the cause. The losing side loses completely. Their jobs are gone and they won't come back. It takes a very strong-willed politician to pass up the short-term benefits of protecting dying industries, when the political benefits from doing so are substantial and the costs are imposed on someone else.

This regulatory disagreement, which turns on an apparently small technical difference between contractors and employees, is important. A contractor, from the Latin verb to draw together different things, brings their own tools and skills, and does a (relatively) brief stint of work in a defined task. An employee, from the Latin verb to be entangled, associated or connected, is someone who predictably works at one job, often using the tools or equipment of the employer, over an indefinite and possibly quite long period.

The difference between the categories matters for the way insurance and benefits are regulated. Companies, workers and legislators are arguing about how to think about the very nature of work. This is clearly good for people who are able to share excess capacity directly: instead of paying for a car and *then* paying to park it at the airport, for example, an app such as Turo operates as a car rental agency and leases out my car for the two weeks I'll be gone on a business trip. I save the cost of paying for parking, and I make some money when someone rents from me instead of Europcar or Sixt.

But in some parts of the sharing economy, you might object, I am not just sharing excess capacity, but also contracting for labour. When I call an Uber, that driver owns or leases that car and has her own driving skills to get me to where I want to go. From the perspective of the rider, the Uber driver is not an employee: I am not hiring the driver to work for me, any more than would be the case for a taxi driver.

One must ask, however, about the relationship between the driver and Uber. True, the driver supplies her own car and driving skills. But there is a much more entangled connection, as Uber supplies information, reputation ratings, insurance, takes the payment from the rider and then pays the driver on a regular weekly schedule. (Uber 'weeks' end at 3.59 a.m. every Monday and the driver is paid a single total sum at 4 a.m.)

Recently, the US state of California passed legislation (AB #5) that tries to clarify the situation. The law states if someone works for pay from a single entity then there is a legal presumption that person is an employee, not a contractor, unless the worker is not controlled by the company, does things outside the company's normal business, and is working in an independently established trade or business. Many app-based businesses that pay people to do tasks, such as Uber, would find themselves regulated by laws that require benefits and control working conditions. Others, such as Airbnb, where the transaction is mostly about the physical space, not the work, might not.

This issue is complex and it is hard to know which side has this right. Interestingly, California is already a world leader in a hybrid kind of employment, the 'gig economy', which might illustrate what is likely to happen in the future. Hollywood films, for example, were once made by the major studios such as Metro-Goldwyn-Mayer or 20th Century Fox. These studios are now distributors. Films are made by 'gig' workers, hired for the duration of the shooting of the film. But in almost all cases, they are contractors, not employees.

The way it works is interesting and surprisingly smooth for something so decentralised. There are about 150 different disciplines involved in making a film, including all those job titles you see at the end of the credits: the gaffer, the key grip and the appealingly titled 'best boy'. If you make a film, you go to LinkedIn and choose one of each of these disciplinary workers. On the first day of shooting, the team works well together because the refinements of division of labour in the industry are clear and well organised. After the film is completed, the gig is over.

That means that some workers, those with specialised skills and established reputations, can make a very substantial living working intensely for only six to eight months each year. But because their work is temporary and their speciality is narrow compared to the scope of work of the employer, they would probably fall outside the new requirements for classification as employees.

The real problem is that we may end up having to choose between two unpalatable options: accept that the gig economy extends even to companies such as Uber, with all the consequent problems for drivers, or decide that we would be better off regulating app-based firms out of existence by requiring them to pay benefits and accept working condition regulations. Uber and Lyft are likely to pull out of California, or at least cut back sharply on their operations. Given how popular and widely used ride-sharing has become, it will be interesting to see if the backlash among riders overwhelms the political resolve of California's political power-brokers. A recent study (Cook et al. 2019) points out an additional problem: the flexibility of the low-skill gig economy is a crucial opportunity for older people with few other employment opportunities. The ability to work flexible hours would be eliminated if regulators forced drivers to be categorised as employees, with all the accompanying rules and requirements for compensation that entails.

The difference between contractors and employees is both legally and practically important. 'Contractors' bring their own tools and skills, and do a stint or 'gig' of work in a defined task. 'Employees' are associated or connected with someone who pays their wages. Employees work at one job, using tools or equipment supplied by the employer, over an indefinite period. This cashes out (literally) as distinctions in legal context, tax rules and regulations that govern how people work.

There are two reasons why the distinction has become of paramount importance recently, and why even well-intentioned attempts at regulation are destructive. The first is the 'sharing economy', the creation of a system where short-term 'gigs' are crucial components to serve customers and allow workers to earn a little extra money. If I'm headed to work in my car, but have a few extra minutes, and you are nearby and need a ride, we can help each other out.

But driving is not my primary job, and riding in cars is not your first love in life. It's just a quick connection, a gig, that makes our day a little better and a little easier. Requiring that gig workers be treated as employees forces many of our poorest and most vulnerable citizens to give up the flexibility and extra pay that can make the difference between getting by and getting lost.

That brings us to the second important reason that regulations that force gig contracts into 'employment' are so dangerous. The situation in early summer 2020, with voluntary (and mandatory) self-isolation, created an immediate need for flexible and low-cost delivery workers. Hiring laws, especially for firms with more than 50 employees, meant that companies were quite reasonably unwilling to make long-term commitments to traditional jobs. No one was sure what our economic needs and capacities were going to be, even two months ahead. But, in these new circumstances, hiring someone in a traditional job, with hours requirements and benefits, is too expensive to contemplate given the employer has no idea whether there will be work.

This comes down to the costs of distributing risk. The intent of regulators, it appears, was to place more of the risk on the hiring company by forcing them to treat gig workers as employees. But the result is that employers are not hiring, and gig workers are unable to take on the myriad tasks that are needed to flatten out the costs of the temporary emergency. It doesn't really matter how great the pay is, how predictable the hours are, and how generous the benefits are, if the law prevents the job from existing in the first place. As it stands, regulations have unintentionally pushed many of the risks and costs of the changing gig economy onto the lower middle class, those who would most benefit from flexibility and those with few resources to work around the restrictive policies.

The policy comparison should not be between 'exploited contractors' and 'good jobs with benefits'; policy must balance the advantages of markets – flexibility and rapid adjustments to new conditions – and the needs of workers for predictability and a sense of security. Fostering a space for robust platforms is a middle ground, making more efficient use of excess capacity through commodification via app-based businesses. Luddism is an understandable political impulse, clinging to what we know. But my argument is that 'protecting jobs' will make the problem much worse and will artificially extend the period of necessary adjustment.

The benefits of commodification and modular temporal access will extend to all citizens, in the form of less need for storage, much lower prices and the ability to live together more comfortably. The insistence on full-time jobs, with benefits, is a crushing tax on precisely those people most in need of short-term gigs and other flexible work arrangements to help them through the transition. Decentralised market processes have two advantages over any central plan or industrial policy: first, each individual can 'plan' his or her own response; second, the speed and breadth of the market dynamics have a robustness that the state cannot hope to mimic. There will be fewer 'jobs', but more 'work' to be done, and to be paid for. If the state doesn't block the market response, platforms can lead the way.

A different example: 'Uber but for planes'

If I am a pilot and have my own aeroplane and I am planning to fly from San Francisco to Portland, Oregon, it would be easy for me to carry an extra passenger and a normal amount of luggage along with me. The fixed costs (the airplane, maintenance, insurance, landing fees, my licence and experience as a pilot) are already paid. The additional cost would be the small amount of additional fuel because of the extra weight.

But of course it is hard for me to find someone who wants to go from the same place to the same place, at the same time. It is hard for us to get together and to arrange the payment. And I am not sure I want to fly with someone I don't know, because they might rob me or just be crazy and creepy.

What is required is a platform that does those three things and does them very fast and without effort by either the pilot or the potential passengers. The developers of Flytenow realised that it could make money by selling reductions in transaction costs in a kind of 'Uber, but for planes' arrangement. In a way, this is very like our earlier discussion of BlaBlaCar in Europe, because this is a trip that the driver/pilot was going to take anyway. So, if the price is equal to the marginal cost, plus just a little, both passenger and pilot are better off.

But, for political reasons, it is tempting for the arbiter to want to play. The fact that there are mutually beneficial exchanges that are now not taking place is less of a concern than the desire of the referee to control everything and the desire of special interests (charter flights and airlines, in this case) to block new ways of doing business. The US Federal Aviation Administration imposed new regulations in early 2016, ignoring the fact that flight-sharing is already widely used, and quite safe, in Europe.[5] The UK, to its credit,

---

5   Justices ground startup Flytenow, the 'Uber of the sky': D.C. Circuit ruling favouring the Federal Aviation Administration, won't be reviewed. *National Law Journal*, 9 January 2017 (https://www.law.com/national lawjournal/almID/1202776363942/Justices-Ground-Startup-Flytenow -the-Uber-of-the-Sky/?cmp=share_twitter&slreturn=20200026102242).

has allowed participation for its airports and citizens in the Wingly platform, which has more than 3,000 private pilots registered in the UK alone, with another 10,000 on the European continent.[6]

Wingly is more like BlaBlaCar (i.e. hitchhiking) than Uber, because you are 'hitching a ride' on a flight the pilot is likely to be taking already. The empty front seat, or several seats, would otherwise be empty. That is the point of sharing: we make more efficient use of existing resources and trips that are already being paid for, while making services available to people who might not otherwise be able to afford them. Regulators are holding back an innovation that will be disruptive to existing ways of doing things, but that is because the way we do things now is deficient. As one of the founders of Flytenow, Alan Guichard, put it:

> ... special interests are at the heart of it. The FAA is being pressured by lobbyists in the private charter and airline arena to ban flight sharing. Why? Because flight sharing gives people options—sharing a flight from Boston to Martha's Vineyard costs less than £70, whereas a charter would cost at least £1,000. These established business models see flight sharing as a threat ...
>
> According to the FAA, it is perfectly okay for strangers who meet over a physical bulletin to share a flight, but if those same people meet online, where flight-sharing

---

6   Wingly: will the 'Uber of the skies' take off? *The Guardian*, 14 July 2018 (https://www.theguardian.com/travel/2018/jul/14/wingly-flight-sharing-channel).

services such as Flytenow offer verified identities, then
the flight magically transforms into an illegal commercial operation.[7]

One of the problems of public policy analysis is that effects
that seem like costs from one perspective are benefits for
someone else. It is precisely because the Uber-style software platform allows people to find each other, to make
payments, and to trust each other – i.e. reduces transaction costs – that it is prohibited. Less efficient, less effective
ways of matching passengers and pilots pass the gimlet
eye of the regulator; the problem is precisely that platforms work better. Regulations are a new form of the same
old impulse that made the mythical Ned Ludd a hero two
centuries ago.

There are other platforms, however, where the UK and
Europe are regulating much more intrusively than the
US, especially in the market for lodging. Several cities,
including Reykjavik, Iceland, have found that regulations to control the use of apartments for Airbnb or other
short-term rental sublet facilitators were needed to stem
a drastic shrinkage in the longer-term rental market. To
the 'seller', the economic logic is compelling: suppose you
can get £1,500 per month for a renter with an annual lease.
But suppose you can get £200 per night for a short vacation
rental, and you can average 20 nights rented per month.
That's £4,000 per month. Of course, until now the second

---

7   Uber for planes. *Forbes*, 31 May 2016 (http://www.forbes.com/sites/jared
     meyer/2016/05/31/uber-for-planes/).

option of several, or many, short-term rentals was blocked by transaction costs. Now, however, it's easily done. An interesting example is described by Kirsten Brown:[8]

> One Airbnb host in Reykjavik told me that converting a rental unit he owned had provided him and his wife with income to save for retirement – something he could never afford to do renting the property out annually.
>
> 'We make maybe two to four times the money depending on the time of the year,' said Heimer Fridriksdottir, who owns one Airbnb unit and is a janitor. 'If it's our apartment, it should be up to us who we rent it to. The city should just build more apartments.'

There is a growing and politically problematic trend towards landlords buying up entire buildings, giving the current tenants non-renewal notices at the end of their leases, and then converting all those units (in effect) to hotels, with Airbnb operating the front desk and reservations line. The problem appears to be particularly acute, or perhaps is just attracting more notice, in the UK. In the summer of 2018, the All-Party Parliamentary Group on Tourism, Leisure and the Hospitality Industry published a white paper that detailed the extent of the problem.

Many people who want to go to London or to a coastal resort on holiday are renting flats or rooms using Airbnb. But according to the white paper, many of the rental units

---

8 Airbnb has made it nearly impossible to find a place to live in this city. *Fusion Online*, 24 May 2016 (http://fusion.kinja.com/airbnb-has-made-it -nearly-impossible-to-find-a-place-to-1793856969).

are actually owned by relatively large, centralised businesses that specialise in rentals full time. The concern is that emergency authorities are not aware of the location or extent of these rental units, which amount to more than 60,000 units in London. When compared with the number of hotel rooms – about 200,000 units – the size of the issue becomes clear. According to a report by the accounting firm Moore Stephens, the ratio (more than a quarter the size of the hotel industry) is similar in Brighton and Bristol.

Gordon Marsden, who was chairman of the parliamentary group and the MP for Blackpool South, said: 'There is an image that this is a lot of happy, jolly people with a spare room trying to make some pin money ... That's true, but it's also true that there seems to be systematic attempts to do block-booking in blocks of flats. That's problematic.'

The report revealed that there were a large number of hosts that listed multiple, and in some cases more than ten, properties and units on Airbnb, in some cases listing most or even all the units in a particular block of flats. As Marsden put it:

> They have their hands on a number of different properties and many of those are often in large tower blocks. That suggests that sharing-economy platforms are increasingly being used to develop tourism accommodation businesses rather than simply renting a room on an ad hoc basis.

This problem has appeared in the past two years in at least twenty cities worldwide – in every case in a setting where there are restrictions on building new housing units and hotels, whether in the form of planning restrictions or licensing delays. In the case of London and New York, the result has been the cannibalising of existing long-term rental units for short-term 'hotel' arrangements.

The tendency is for state regulators, as shown by the indignation of Mr Marsden, to 'solve' the problem by piling on additional regulations, restricting Airbnb. But the real price signal being sent is that there is not enough housing. The artificial restrictions on new construction are really the driving force behind Airbnb being used in this way. On the flip side of that shortage is the occasional surplus of hotel rooms, which the existing system has difficulty commoditising and using for slightly longer-term stays. This idle capacity could often be available for some other use if the platform were more flexible.

In the case of London, there is an increasing stock of finished but unsold new luxury housing,[9] at the same time that the number of 'affordable' flats is shrinking. The proliferation of Airbnb units is a symptom rather than the cause of the underlying problem, which is government restrictions on the construction of new housing. Top-end developers are more able to pay the costs of overcoming NIMBY[10] pressures and planning delays. But affordable housing in middle-class neighbourhoods is largely shut

---

9 London's stockpile of unsold homes jumps to an all-time high. *Bloomberg*, 20 November 2018 (https://www.bloomberg.com/news/articles/2018-11 -20/london-s-stockpile-of-unsold-homes-jumps-almost-50-to-a-record).

10 'Not in my back yard.'

down. This creates a rent premium and the conversion of flats to Airbnb hotels is an unintended consequence.

Nonetheless, the solution is to work to checkmate NIMBY vetoes, rather than veto the Airbnb activity, which actually increases availability for visitors and people on holiday to cities and resorts. The Airbnb example is indicative, in fact, of the larger problem: high property prices generally indicate problems with regulatory structure. But regulatory authorities rarely recognise their own responsibility, or at a minimum complicity, in creating the problems in the first place. The temptation is always to slather on a new layer of even more distortionary regulations and to blame greed and market failure for problems largely created by ill-formed state policies.

Fairness, exclusion and 'social credit'

Earlier the difficulty of reconceiving problems of antitrust or monopolies was discussed, though only superficially. There is a larger and deeper problem, one that will challenge public policy in ways that current conceptions of economic regulation are ill-equipped to address. The notion of fairness is more than a matter of abstract social justice; access to the mechanics of the sharing economy is a requirement for the system to achieve the kind of widely shared dynamic growth pointed to by its advocates. And the exclusion of some participants means that the opportunities for innovation that make such a system attractive will be missed.

There are two aspects of the 'exclusion' problem, one at the level of new entrants at the firm/app level and the other at the participant/consumer level. I will consider each in turn.

- *Firms and apps.* The most obvious problem, discussed in an earlier chapter, is the difficulty of overcoming entry barriers in selling 'trust'. It is likely that it will be possible to design improved apps and user connections for some of the core 'sharing' services such as transport or housing. But even if a new app is better on other margins of convenience, it will be very difficult to collect a portfolio of rides or properties with enough reviews to ensure a reliable and safe service. Given the choice between an older, less convenient app and a shiny new app with no reviews, many and perhaps most potential customers will stick with the old app. Uber has accumulated a huge stock of crowdsourced trust and it will be very difficult for any start-up to overcome that advantage.
- *Individuals and 'social credit'.* Consumers, renters and users also face the problem of asymmetric information. It is common in insurance and other industries where adverse selection is a problem to look for some mechanism for sorting consumers by risk classification. If these sorting mechanisms are effective, they can actually change behaviour and make the whole system operate more cheaply and efficiently.

There is a potential problem, in terms of the loss of privacy that comes from being monitored for safe behaviour.

A number of British providers of car insurance provide discounts for the installation and use of gadgets such as dashcams or parking sensors. Drivers who install such cameras, or devices that monitor speed and the aggressiveness of driving habits, are giving up their anonymity; many devices even record the time and location of stops, or save a record of driving routes, speeds and time spent at various places for the entire day. A survey conducted by Bodyshop Business[11] found that drivers didn't mind giving up their privacy; the most common objection was that the discount drivers received – about £28 – was too small. After all, the saving to the insurance company can be substantial and the consequent incentive to drivers to adjust their behaviour can make the saving even greater if the benefits are shared.

More generally, it does seem that there should be some means of making reputations portable. If an owner of a flat has an excellent and reliable record on Airbnb, it is likely to translate into trustworthiness in getting a loan or care in driving a car. The causation could go in the other direction: if having a bad credit rating or being a reckless driver negatively affected one's Airbnb host rating, then the person in question may be judged to be a 'good' citizen in all aspects of his or her life. And that is exactly the peril – to go along with the promise – of such general 'social credit scores'. If the costs of everything we pay to use are adjusted by risk premiums or good behaviour discounts, then almost all

---

11 British drivers expect insurance discounts for safety gadgets. *Bodyshop Business*, 12 July 2016 (https://www.bodyshopbusiness.com/british-driv ers-expect-insurance-discounts-for-safety-gadgets/).

of our actions must be recorded and (more ominously) judged and scored for conformity to social norms.

China's 'social credit score' has produced widespread controversy, often because it is poorly understood. As Nicol Kobie[12] puts it, 'China's social credit system has been compared to [the television series] *Black Mirror* ... and every other dystopian future sci-fi writers can think up. The reality is more complicated – and in some ways, worse'. Sophie Gilbert, writing about the *Black Mirror* episode 'Nosedive' in particular,[13] notes that if you accept the unexplained premise of retinal implants that superimpose digital information on people around you, the connection between a person and his or her 'history' becomes public. 'The minute you see someone you can also see their ranking, meaning that reality has morphed into a pastel-colored nightmare of aggressive cheeriness, as citizens attempt to out-nice each other and bump up their ratings'.

A more serious (and non-fictional) perspective is offered in Lilico and Sinclair (2016):

> The sharing economy has the potential to encompass a significant portion of economic and social life; and this might create a danger of a new (and potentially rather comprehensive) form of social exclusion. Users of certain

---

12 The complicated truth about China's social credit system. *Wired UK*, 7 June 2019 (https://www.wired.co.uk/article/china-social-credit-system -explained).

13 *Black Mirror*'s 'Nosedive' skewers social media. *The Atlantic*. 21 October 2016 (https://www.theatlantic.com/entertainment/archive/2016/10/black -mirror-nosedive-review-season-three-netflix/504668/).

sharing economy platforms whose reputational ratings fall below key thresholds are excluded from the platform. Those so excluded may find it impossible to re-enter the platform to rebuild their reputation, because they cannot update their scores once they are excluded.

There is also some risk that users could become excluded maliciously or frivolously. These risks should be addressed from a public policy perspective.

It is tempting to want state regulation and control of exclusion, to prevent misuse of the power to withhold access to reputation scores and misuse of the power they encompass. At the time of writing, there is substantial public sentiment in favour of 'contact tracing', isolating and tracking the movements of individuals who have been exposed to the Covid-19 virus, for example. But it is at least as likely that the misuse of this power will be centred in the state, as a mechanism of social control. Reputation and trust in the private sector are built on reliability and trustworthiness; trust in politics can be broken by simple acts of dissent or honest disagreement. I cannot pretend to resolve this tension in this short publication, but it is worth highlighting the concern in all its frustrating ambiguity.

8   CONCLUSION

Platforms help human societies nurture and support co-operation, and have been essential as long as there have been societies. Some platforms, such as feudal city-states, solved the problems of triangulation, transfer and trust by organising hierarchy and issuing commands. This arrangement allowed important advances in artistic achievement, military technology and tactics, plant and animal domestication, and population growth. Hierarchy allowed the exploitation of division of labour on a scale that up to that point had been unthinkable.

But there was always pressure to cooperate not just within, but across city-states and smaller geopolitical units. Cooperation across units requires markets. The transition from hunter-gatherer societies to city-states could be accomplished in command systems, and that was enough to support the first great explosion in human population and civilisation, the beginnings of the accumulation of knowledge and advances in techniques of metallurgy and tool-making. But wealth, the real wealth that results from the division of labour, requires much larger populations and a price mechanism to guide decentralised activity. As Adam Smith put it, division of labour is limited by the extent of the market. Markets want to be global, in the sense that larger populations and greater specialisation tend to promote wealth creation.

There is a great obstacle to the smooth functioning of markets, operating like the friction sand causes in a motor. That obstacle is transaction costs, a problem solved internally by hierarchy but which across units requires additional institutions. Platforms are institutions that solve the problems of identifying opportunity, of delivering the good or service and clearing the payment, and in trusting. They have always been important, from the souks of the Middle East 3,000 years ago to the Sears catalogue of the nineteenth century to Amazon today. The difference is that now platforms have become an end in themselves, resulting in the effective commodification of excess capacity.

Such innovation changes everything. It makes excess capacity modular so it can be bought and sold as if it were copper on the London Commodities Exchange. As it stands, we pay for most durables twice: first the capital cost, which then stands idle most of the time, and second for the storage, which in cities is becoming more and more expensive. Neither of these costs is efficient, because once we get past empty symbols of elite status we may not intrinsically want to own and store things.[1] The product we pay for and then store is mostly wasted. If we can share, we

[1] The striving for status, of course, is something deeply ingrained in the human psyche. But the symbols that confer status are something societies create. We can already see a generational change in this direction, in part driven by platforms. If you look at my social media feed, you'll see pictures of my house, or my car, or other physical things. If you view my sons' social media, you'll see experiences: hang-gliding in Nepal, or snorkelling in Bermuda. Both sets of images confer status, but young people are already making the substitution, choosing *doing things* over *owning things*.

can get more use, of better things, at less cost, and have a lot more room to go along with all that extra money.

While much of the description in this book has been optimistic, mostly pointing out likely positives, there may also be a darker side. The inequalities created by virtual platforms, in commodities and consumer products, in jobs, and in services, are a real concern. Change is not easy, but we are going to have to deal with it.

Change as a constant

In the biosphere, there is always a tension between being specifically adapted to a particular environmental niche and being able to respond to change. Given enough time, evolutionary change as a result of natural selection will optimise any living organism, but there is no 'best' answer, if only because a sudden change in underlying conditions can be catastrophic. The dinosaurs thrived until an asteroid strike changed the weather so much and so quickly that they were unable to adapt in time. Mammals, in contrast, were better able to survive and adapt to the new conditions because of their smaller size, fur coats and fast metabolism.

In the long run, the ability to adapt to change is the key to survival. The difference is that human societies can choose, unlike animals, to build flexibility and responsiveness into statutes and regulations. Social systems must be able to serve people in periods of stability, by creating predictable patterns of rules and expectations, and to serve people in times of disruption, by fostering innovation and entrepreneurship without breaking down.

On a larger scale, competition *among* societies and innovation *within* societies generates change that has to be mediated by institutions. As Knight (1992) pointed out, these institutions are often the products of the need to generate stability and predictability. Managing fundamental change takes a lot of attention and energy, but it rewards the creative spark.

The Ottoman Empire lasted for more than 600 years; it was stable and internally peaceful. But this stability was purchased at the price of economic stagnation and retarded scientific progress in a dozen nations. As Kuran (2011) argues, stability and coherence alone are not enough. On the other hand, the activities of Enron Corporation showed that rapid adaptation, moving ahead of the ability of market institutions or property rights to adjust, can be catastrophic (Maclean and Elkind 2004).

The Industrial Revolution wiped out social and cultural institutions and traditions on a wide scale. Some analysts are now arguing that we are on the threshold of similarly disruptive changes. The nature of work, our sources of income, and the way we own and use things may be profoundly different in just a few decades.

Change and its revolutionary consequences have long been a central concern of social theorists. In human civilisations, disruptive changes are often endogenous, generated internally by the Schumpeterian process of creative destruction in capitalism. Marx believed that these 'crises' would eventually destroy capitalism, as wrenching change evoked revolution. To be fair, Marx and Engels [1848] (1969) were quite right when they claimed that:

> For many a decade past the history of industry and commerce is but the history of the revolt of modern productive forces against modern conditions of production, against the property relations that are the conditions for the existence of the bourgeois and of its rule. It is enough to mention the commercial crises that by their periodical return put the existence of the entire bourgeois society on its trial, each time more threateningly. In these crises, a great part not only of the existing products but also of the previously created productive forces, are periodically destroyed. In these crises, there breaks out an epidemic that, in all earlier epochs, would have seemed an absurdity – the epidemic of over-production.

Over long periods, 'over-production' is actually what we call 'wealth'; it's good, not bad. It is still true, however, just as Marx believed, that the effects on parts of society are powerfully damaging. Existing jobs and ways of doing business are wiped out, often unexpectedly.

Joseph Schumpeter agreed, in part, but saw this as being not a drawback, but rather one of the chief arguments *for* capitalism (Schumpeter 1942: 82–83):

> Captalism ... is by nature a form or method of economic change and not only never is but never can be stationary. And this evolutionary character of the capitalist process is not merely due to the fact that economic life goes on in a social and natural environment which changes and by its change alters the data of economic action; this fact is important and these changes (wars, revolutions and so

on) often condition industrial change, but they are not its prime movers.

Nor is this evolutionary character due to a quasi-automatic increase in population and capital or to the vagaries of monetary systems of which exactly the same thing holds true. The fundamental impulse that sets and keeps the capitalist engine in motion comes from the *new consumers' goods, the new methods of production or transportation, the new markets, the new forms of industrial organization that capitalist enterprise creates* [emphasis added].

It is all very exciting. We can see it happening around us, as products and services that once did not exist or were available only to the wealthy are now available universally and practically free of charge.

Saltation

One kind of disruption, which in my book *Tomorrow 3.0* I called 'saltation', is mostly – though not entirely – good. Unlike biological evolution, which is gradual and slow, cultural evolution has a Lamarckian aspect[2] and so economic revolutions can be discontinuous and dramatic. In practice, this means that the institutional and legal preconditions for development in poor nations no longer need to go through a series of dreary and time-consuming

2   While Lamarck's 'inheritance of acquired characteristics' is not consistent with biological genetic mutation, social and institutional evolution is a much more congenial setting for his ideas.

stages; ideas can be replicated around the world at low cost, driven by mimicry and aspiration of the sort envisioned by J.-B. Lamarck (1809: chapters VI and VII, pp. 68–127).

Much of what we think we know about development, entrepreneurship and the function of government and markets is based on certain assumptions about institutions and preconditions. Software will allow even a nation with a corrupt government and police force, rudimentary banks and broken capital markets to produce useful services. Development economists have long told developing nations that they must follow a particular path of rule of law, independent judiciary, financial system, and so on. This essentially material, marginalist notion of 'stages' of development is clear in Marx, who said, 'The country that is more developed industrially only shows, to the less developed, the image of its own future' (Marx 1867).

But what if blockchain apps and cryptocurrency could simply operate on top of a corrupt system? Turn-key capitalism! Functioning markets in a box – or an 'app', at least! The reduction in prices, and an increasing variety of services and activities available free of charge or for a very low cost, are likely to provide a platform for leapfrogging the traditional stages of development and the usual institutions required for starting and running a business. This jumping will disrupt the banks, the courts and the political entities that try to control business activities, but it will also allow people to become competitive in nations that lack financial intermediaries, a system of law and state capacity to provide infrastructure.

Separation

The other kind of disruption, which is already commonly called 'separation', is mostly – though not entirely – bad, because it means that many people will be left behind, in most cases through no particular fault of their own, and will be relegated to second-class status in wealthy nations.

I am not convinced that separation is inevitable; much of the discussion of the stagnation of the total compensation of the middle class has ignored the dramatic decline in prices for many goods and services, especially online platforms such as Facebook, Twitter and Wikipedia. Still, it is true that software is replacing a lot of service jobs, and this may continue for years to come.

I have argued that the key feature of the new economy is the commodification of excess capacity. Like the commodification of labour in the eighteenth and nineteenth centuries, this may result at first in a stretching of the income distribution. Those without programming skills and who do not have durables, such as cars for Uber or houses for Airbnb, may find themselves in a difficult position economically.

The three most important impacts of the new sharing economy are likely to be:

- A dramatic reduction in the amount of physical stuff, in the form of consumer durables, being produced in factories by workers.
- An equally dramatic decline in the cost of having access to a variety of stuff and a sharp reduction in costs of storage.

- An ambiguous, but unsettling, effect on real wages, with both the direction and variance of real wages very much in flux.

Over the last twenty years, two things have happened in US manufacturing. The total number of jobs in manufacturing has fallen from about 18 million to just over 10 million; for the UK, the total fell from 3.8 million jobs in 2000 to just over 2.5 million today.[3] But the total value of manufacturing has increased steadily. This increase in productivity is good.

The problem is that it means that there are fewer people working in these kinds of jobs. In the past, the service sector has taken up the slack, but it is not clear that will happen this time. After all, software has the same effects on service jobs that robots and automation have had on manufacturing jobs.

I do not have a crystal ball and I have shown in the past that I am terrible at making predictions. But if there is a way to encourage saltation, because it levels the differences between developed and less developed nations, we should explore it. And if there are ways to mitigate the harmful political effects of separation, we should explore those too.

As was discussed in the previous chapter, attempts to use restrictive work requirements and minimum wages have understandable, even laudable, objectives. But their actual consequences are harmful to the very people that advocates

---

3   For the US data, see the BLS (2020); for the UK data, see Rhodes (2020).

purport to want to help. Platforms replace traditional employment contracts, and attempts to preserve traditional employment will artificially hasten that process.

The events of the past year show an additional advantage of platforms, a feature that many observers have rightly decried as a drawback. Platforms take out the 'human element' of many of our purchases. Where once we had to rely on names, and relationships, and personal knowledge, now we can rely on algorithms and systems. But in a world where concerns about contacts and contagion have come to the fore, platforms may get an unexpected boost. And that brings us to the final consideration of this chapter: innovation.

The general answer: permissionless innovation

The general answer for policy implications is frustratingly vague – what I call permissionless innovation (Munger 2017). Friedrich Schiller, the German philosopher and poet, described his vision of the beauty of the 'Englische Tanze' (English Dance) in a letter to a friend in 1793 (Wilkinson and Willoughby 1967: 153):

> I know of no better image for the ideal of a beautiful society than a well-executed English dance, composed of many complicated figures and turns. A spectator located on the balcony observes an infinite variety of criss-crossing motions which keep decisively but arbitrarily changing directions without ever colliding with each other. Everything has been arranged in such a manner that each dancer has

already vacated his position by the time the other arrives. Everything fits so skilfully, yet so spontaneously, that everyone seems to be following his own lead, without ever getting in anyone's way. Such a dance is the perfect symbol of one's own individually asserted freedom as well as of one's respect for the freedom of the other.

Schiller intends more than admiration for the lovely patterns that emerge in the dance; he intends this image to be understood as a metaphor for human society.

The best way to describe the image is a system with plenty of room for saltation, in a context where separation is limited because everyone can participate. As Thierer (2014) points out, one way to define permissionless innovation as a guide to public policy is simply a strong presumption in favour of allowing experimentation with new technologies and new business platforms that use those technologies.

This may seem like common sense, but it is not. For decades in the US, the Bell Telephone network refused to connect any phones except those that it licensed. The claim was that the phones might not be safe, but the effect was to arrest progress at the stage of rotary phones attached by wires to walls. The problem went far beyond phone sets, though. Hazlett (2017) argues that requiring permission (to use frequency) set back US communication innovation by decades.

There are two kinds of obstacles to permissionless innovation: requiring permission from competitors and requiring permissions from regulators. The first seems absurd, since by definition most innovations harm competitors; that is what makes them innovations (Stossel 2017). The second type of obstacle, needing permission from regulators, seems more innocuous. But it is not. The delays in processing applications for permission to experiment sharply curtail the types and frequency of experiments that are possible. Worse, attempts by regulators to pick winners and losers can pose obstacles of their own. Authorities may not require licences for technological experiments, but they do often try to pick winners by offering subsidies to the kinds of work that strike them as 'promising'.

Of course, the very nature of innovation means that it is often the least 'promising' technologies – in the view of 'experts' – that turn out to be the most important. A Yale management professor famously told student Fred Smith that '[t]he concept is interesting and well-formed, but in order to earn better than a "C", the idea must be feasible'. The idea of Federal Express may have got a 'C' from Yale, but it got an 'A+' once it was actually implemented.

In that instance the 'permission of competitors' and 'permission of regulators' came down to the same body: the US Postal Service. FedEx was allowed to slip through only because there was a loophole for 'extremely urgent' letters and parcels.[4] And that's the reason that 'Extremely Urgent' still appears on every envelope FedEx delivers.

We are on the brink of a new golden age of permission-less innovation. The internet on its own is an infrastructure where a bewildering variety of innovations can be tried out – and (almost) all of these experiments can be

---

4   Suspension for extremely urgent letters. Code of Federal Regulations, 39 CFR § 320 (https://www.law.cornell.edu/cfr/text/39/320.6).

conducted without getting anyone's permission. Think for a second what an inane idea Twitter is; nobody is going to spend any time writing short messages and even fewer people are going to read them. What is it? This is how Ev Williams, an early founder, described it:

> With Twitter, it wasn't clear what it was. They called it a social network, they called it microblogging, but it was hard to define, because it didn't replace anything. There was this path of discovery with something like that, where over time you figure out what it is. Twitter actually changed from what we thought it was in the beginning, which we described as status updates and a social utility. It is that, in part, but the insight we eventually came to was Twitter was really more of an information network than it is a social network.[5]

The analogy to the dance is quite clear: access to the internet spawned an innovation called Twitter, but no one knew what it was for. Then, before long, people worked out a use for Twitter, because once it was there, they could experiment without asking for anyone's permission. No one, not even Twitter's own founders, understood what would make it useful.

I have previously speculated about how Friedrich Schiller might put it, if he saw Twitter today (Munger 2017):

---

5   Ev Williams on Twitter's early years. 4 October 2013 (https://www.inc
    .com/issie-lapowsky/ev-williams-twitter-early-years.html?cid=em01011
    week40day04b).

A spectator following a hashtag observes an infinite variety of criss-crossing tweets which keep decisively but arbitrarily changing directions without ever censoring each other. Everything fits so skilfully, yet so spontaneously, that everyone seems to be following his own lead, but the thread builds into an informative whole without any guidance or central direction. Such an app is the perfect symbol of one's own individually asserted freedom to convey useful truths, as well as of one's respect for the freedom of the other to post random cat videos.

Economic revolutions don't care what we think of them. Both problems and solutions will come from unexpected directions, because the platform revolution is now being given some welly in nearly every aspect of our lives. In 2030, the frictions and legacy institutions that dominate the economy in 2021 will not look the same, and many of them won't even exist.

But there may be one positive aspect to the economic chaos and destruction that seems to surround us. Mancur Olson (1982) famously argued that nations' economies and vitality are sapped by what he called 'institutional sclerosis'. Interest groups attach themselves, leech-like, to the arteries of commerce and value creation, and eventually a vibrant national culture grows benumbed and inert. Olson observed that one means of stripping away all of these parasites and hangers-on was war; it was the utter destruction of the interest-group ecosystems of Japan and Germany, on this account, that explain their post-war economic success. Olson doesn't recommend destruction as a policy measure, but he notes that the accretion of unions, lobbyists and concentrated interests is otherwise hard to prevent.

Final words: the next three crises

It is useful to offer some closing speculations, if only briefly, about what the likely policy problems will be for a changing platform economy in the next decade. There appear to be three distinct but connected challenges for legislators and regulators: the effects of (a) *the Covid-19 pandemic*, (b) *information ownership and antitrust*, and (c) *reconceiving (un)employment*.

There are reasons to be optimistic. For one thing, it is at least possible that regulatory authorities will conceive and implement a comprehensive response that addresses all three, with nimble and decentralised empowerment of the resources that permissionless innovation in platforms makes possible. But even if that is not true, there is an optimistic alternative: a crisis that moves us forward. The increasingly strident last-ditch defences of the dirigiste regimes that have dominated the UK and Europe may well bring down the system of price control and planning faster than any policy of reform.

How is *that* optimistic? As Milton Friedman (1982: xi) famously pointed out, it is precisely the most spectacular economic cock-ups that produce policy reforms. Well, actually, Friedman said it rather more formally:

> Only a crisis – actual or perceived – produces real change. When that crisis occurs, the actions that are taken

depend on the ideas that are lying around. That, I believe, is our basic function: to develop alternatives to existing policies, to keep them alive and available until the politically impossible becomes the politically inevitable.

It is the urgent task of those of us who see the coming crisis to begin now to create that coherent response that the political system is unlikely to provide. In closing, then, I'll briefly consider the likely impact of each of those three connected challenges.

The *Covid-19 pandemic* has accelerated some aspects of the shift to platforms, but it has also deflected social and cultural norms in unexpected directions. Remote working and 'gig' work make the sort of contract work discussed in chapter 7 of this book much more likely, and create substantial problems for the impulse of many regulators to require fixed work schedules and full-time employment, with benefits. Another dramatic shift, already visible over the past decade but now accelerating with incredible speed, is the shift away from bricks-and-mortar retail of products, services and food, moving towards delivery.

Even in settings where customers still physically visit, the pandemic has accelerated the trend towards self-service. Supermarkets save labour costs, and increase social distancing, by 'allowing' customers to scan and bag their own groceries. If you stop by for a cheeky Nando's, you are likely to find that the person behind the cash register has been transformed into a kiosk. Two years ago you looked at the overhead board and read off the names of dishes and drinks, and the person behind the counter pressed buttons with the corresponding words printed on them. Now restaurants have 'turned the cash register around', so that you press the buttons and pay by inserting a chip card. Fewer people, less contact and delivery all mean less contagion, but they also mean far fewer service jobs, in an economy where such positions were already starting to disappear.

Regulatory policy targeted at locking down the spread of the virus has made the prospects of moving back to service personnel less likely, over and above the economic logic. If another pandemic strikes, the investment in contactless ordering and delivery will pay for itself immediately. And schools and universities, which have discovered that some aspects of the delivery of education can work quite well remotely, are likewise on a permanently different footing regarding format and scale.

Of course, it is precisely the concentration of the delivery of communication, information and entertainment in platforms that makes the second major issue, *information ownership and antitrust*, so central. Traditionally, at least in the UK/US common tradition, bigness alone has not been a crime. The idea of monopoly had more to do with behaviour than market share, though European Union regulatory authorities have debated whether size alone is an offence (Chee and MacDonald 2014).

But recent events have called this doctrine, referred to as 'consumer welfare' antitrust, into question. As chronicled by Kovacic and Shapiro (2000), antitrust policy generally – but particularly in the US and the UK – was transformed over the period 1890–1990 from a muddled conception of biases and suspicions into a coherent perspective on the need to reduce barriers to competition and outlaw contracts in restraint of trade. The 'offence' of bigness in economic firms is the use of market power to restrict output and raise prices, damaging consumer welfare. Harm to other market participants, particularly superior quality or efficiency that drives other firms out of the market, is not only not a problem, but is the point of the creative destruction process that harnesses permissionless innovation for the good of consumers.

Recently, the notion that size alone is a problem, and that even market power secured by network economies and superior performance should be illegal, has re-emerged as an animating force for populist politics and regulatory activism (Manne and Wright 2011; Dorsey et al. 2020). Some of this impulse originates on the political left, in concern about control over personal data (Facebook, Google) or access to products and services (Airbnb, Amazon, Uber). But the recent 'deplatforming' of Donald Trump and an array of others on the political right has led also to concern among conservatives.

This impulse to control and direct innovation and economic activity is not limited to commentators in the legacy and social media. The staff of the Democratic majority of the US House Judiciary Subcommittee on Antitrust, Commercial and Administrative Law spent two years preparing justifications for aggressive action against large platforms, and their report was issued on 29 October 2020 (for an overview, see Kovacic and Sokol 2021). The focus of the inquiry was Amazon, Apple, Facebook and Google; the interesting thing is the recommendation of the report (Majority Staff 2020: 391):

> [T]he Subcommittee recommends that Congress consider reasserting the original intent and broad goals of the antitrust laws, by clarifying that they are designed to protect not just consumers, but also workers, entrepreneurs, independent businesses, open markets, a fair economy, and democratic ideals.

This goes rather far beyond throwing out the sensible and established consumer welfare standard, seeking to restore the 'original intent' of antitrust, specifically highlighting 'democratic ideals'. This kind of populist paroxysm, coming from the very highest levels of the government structures empowered to promulgate regulations, is a radical shift.

Platforms are disruptive, but outlawing disruption has never worked. The problem is that democratic societies are obliged, in the populist conception at least, to implement the impulses of majorities, and more than a few demagogic politicians are happy to take up the populist banner. Worse, in the case of the platforms that have achieved Brobdingnagian stature in the past ten years, there really are unsolved problems of how to think about, much less solve, the challenges posed by centralised ownership and control of personal data and the capacity to censor and deplatform. Things in this arena are likely to get worse before they get better.

Finally, *(un)employment and the 'living wage'*. There have been substantial agitations, in many nations, for a 'living wage' for workers. The premise seems solid: if workers can't live on the pay they receive in their jobs, the system of jobs is not likely to survive. The implications of the developments detailed in this book make it clear, however, that the current system of jobs is not going to survive. The question is not how to prop the system up with neo-Luddite regulations, and wage and price controls, but rather how to ease and, if anything, speed the transition.

Newly elected US President Joe Biden campaigned on raising the minimum wage to $15 – more than £10 – per hour; the UK recently raised its minimum wage to nearly £9 per hour. There are legitimate questions about whether, in the economy of the 2000s, effective minimum wages had substantial impacts on employment.[6]

More broadly, attempts to regulate the terms of employment, lashing down work and hour arrangements that are already anachronistic in many industries, are likewise both politically popular and an awful idea. The recent experience of the US state of California, with its on-again, off-again imposition of restrictions on contractor vs. employee work rules, is indicative of the tendency of a regulator to want to fight the last war instead of reimagining what

---

6   But tying wages to employment in an effort to redistribute income downwards, in a platform economy where the shift to software and kiosks is already being hastened by the Covid-19 pandemic, is sheer political cynicism. Though see Neumark and Shirley (2021), who find that even in the current system the effects of minimum wages have sharply increased barriers to beginning employment for the least advantaged. An alternative way to think about the problem is the problem of local political power as a protection for regulatory rents; see Weingast (1995) on the general effects of fostering competition among jurisdictions as a means of limiting local barriers to employment.

work means. The damage to most workers was easy to predict (Pofeldt 2019), and the almost immediate exemption of many ride-share and other workers from the law's effects by popular referendum (Nastasi 2020) undid much of the damage. But thousands of contractors who had depended on flexible hours and extra income found themselves unable to work.

As De Ruyter et al. (2018) note, the regulatory response must accept that wrenching change and a new way of conceiving of jobs is mandatory. One set of policies will need to deal with what De Ruyter and coauthors call 'labor displacement and reskilling'. But even more broadly, they note (De Ruyter et al. 2018: 37; emphasis mine):

> The second change is the *very nature of work and workplaces*. There will be more work located away from designated workplaces and more work that involves interaction with information and communication technologies. The third change will be regulatory, as work will become 'invisible' and geographically dispersed through online and subcontracting arrangements. For governments there will be challenges regulating employment, identifying employers, collecting taxes, and supporting social protections.

This was written well before the global pandemic, of course, but the need for social distancing has made the problems more, not less, difficult to deal with. The global economy slumped, and unleashing the power of permissionless innovation operating over platforms will be required for any meaningful recovery. Those of us who have been aware of the changes already happening (see, for example, Hazlett 2020) in the new platform economy hope to be able to suggest an alternative to the legacy conventions of antitrust restrictions and propping up wages. Because, like it or not, the economic logic is irresistible, and platforms are aggressively suggesting themselves.

REFERENCES

Arthur, W. B. (1999) Complexity and the economy. *Science* 284: 107–9.

Barzel, Y. (1989) *Economic Analysis of Property Rights*. Cambridge University Press.

Berg, N. (2016) Lots to lose: how cities around the world are eliminating car parks. *The Guardian*, 27 September 2016 (https://www.theguardian.com/cities/2016/sep/27/cities-eliminating-car-parks-parking).

BLS (2020) Bureau of Labor Statistics (https://data.bls.gov/).

Boettke, P. and Candela, R. (2017) The liberty of progress: increasing returns, institutions, and entrepreneurship. *Social Philosophy & Policy* 34(2): 136–63.

Cairncross, F. (1999) *The Death of Distance: How the Communications Revolution Will Change Our Lives*. Cambridge, MA: Harvard Business Press.

Chee, F. Y. and MacDonald, A. (2014) New EU antitrust head not swayed by anti-Americanism, bullies. Reuters (https://www.reuters.com/article/us-eu-antitrust-vestager/new-eu-antitrust-head-not-swayed-by-anti-americanism-bullies-idUSKCN0HI26L20140923).

Cheung, S. N. S. (1973) The fable of the bees: an economic investigation. *Journal of Law and Economics* 16: 11–33.

Cheung, S. N. S. (1998) The transaction cost paradigm. *Economic Inquiry* 36(4): 514–21.

Coase, R. (1937) The nature of the firm. *Economica* 4(16): 386–405.

Coase, R. (2002) *The Intellectual Portrait Series: A Conversation with Ronald H. Coase* (Richard Epstein, interviewer). Indianapolis: Liberty Fund (http://oll.libertyfund.org/titles/979).

Cohen, D. (2018) Tales from the storage unit: inside a booming industry. *Financial Times*.

Cook, C., Diamond, R. and Oyer, P. (2019) Older workers and the gig economy. AEA Papers and Proceedings 109: 372–76.

Demsetz, H. (1967) Toward a theory of property rights. *American Economic Review* 57(2): 347–59.

De Ruyter, A., Brown, M. and Burgess, J. (2018) Gig work and the fourth industrial revolution: conceptual and regulatory challenges. *Journal of International Affairs* 72(1): 37–50.

Dorsey, E., Geoffrey, A. M., Rybnicek, J. M., Stout, K. and Wright, J. D. (2020) Consumer welfare & the rule of law: the case against the new populist antitrust movement. *Pepperdine Law Review* 47: 861–916.

Eckhardt, G. M. and Bardhi, F. (2015) The sharing economy isn't about sharing at all. *Harvard Business Review* (https://hbr.org/2015/01/the-sharing-economy-isnt-about-sharing-at-all).

Emmett, B. and Jeuck, J. E. (1965) *Catalogues and Counters: A History of Sears, Roebuck & Company*. University of Chicago Press.

English Housing Survey (2015) Households: annual report on England's households, 2013–14. July 2015, Revised September 2015. London: Department for Communities and Local Government.

Evans, D. and Schmalensee, R. (2016) *Matchmakers: The New Economics of Multisided Platforms*. Cambridge, MA: Harvard Business Review Press.

Frenken, K. and Schor, J. (2017) Putting the sharing economy into perspective. *Environmental Innovation and Societal Transitions* 23: 3–10.

Frenken, K., Meelen, T., Arets, M. and van de Glind, P. (2015) Smarter regulation for the sharing economy. *The Guardian*, 20.

Friedman, M. (1982) *Capitalism and Freedom* (2002 40th Anniversary Edition). University of Chicago Press.

Ge, Y., Knittel, C. R., MacKenzie, D. and Zoepf, S. (2016) Racial and gender discrimination in transportation network companies. NBER Working Paper 22776.

Guzman, R. A. and Munger, M. C. (2019) A theory of just market exchange. *Journal of Value Inquiry* 54: 1–28.

Harari, Y. (2015) *Sapiens: A Brief History of Humankind*. New York: Harper and Row.

Hardin, G. (1968) The tragedy of the commons. *Science* 162: 1243–48.

Hayek, F. A. (1988) *The Fatal Conceit: The Errors of Socialism*. University of Chicago Press.

Hazlett, T. W. (2017) We could have had cellphones four decades earlier. *Reason Magazine*, July 2017 (http://reason.com/archives/2017/06/11/we-could-have-had-cellphones-f).

Hazlett, T. W. (2020) U.S. antitrust policy in the age of Amazon, Google, Microsoft, Apple, Netflix and Facebook (SSRN: https://ssrn.com/abstract=3594934 or http://dx.doi.org/10.2139/ssrn.3594934).

Howells, G. (2020) Protecting consumer protection values in the fourth industrial revolution. *Journal of Consumer Policy* 43: 145–75 (https://link.springer.com/article/10.1007/s10603-019-09430-3).

Hume, D. [1740] (1896) *A Treatise of Human Nature*, Book 3, Part 2, Section 2. Of the Origin of Justice and Property, Section 7, Of the Origin of Government. Oxford: Clarendon Press (https://oll.libertyfund.org/titles/hume-a-treatise-of-human -nature).

Karolevitz, R. F. (1968) *This Was Pioneer Motoring: An Album of Nostalgic Automobilia*. Seattle, WA: Superior Publishing Co.

Keech, W. R. and Munger, M. C. (2015) The anatomy of government failure. *Public Choice* 164(1–2): 1–42.

Kiesling, L. L. (2016) Implications of smart grid innovation for organizational models in electricity distribution. *Smart Grid Handbook*, 1–15.

Kirzner, I. (1978) Economics and error. In *New Directions in Austrian Economics* (ed. L. M. Spadaro). Mission, KA: Sheed Andrews and McMeel.

Klein, P. G. (2005) The make-or-buy decision: lessons from empirical studies. In *Handbook of New Institutional Economics* (ed. C. Menard and M. Shirley), pp. 435–64. New York: Springer.

Knight, J. (1992) *Institutions and Social Conflict*. Cambridge University Press.

Kovacic, W. E. and Shapiro, C. (2000) Antitrust policy: a century of economic and legal thinking. *Journal of Economic Perspectives* 14: 44–46.

Kovacic, W. E. and Sokol, D. (2021) Understanding the House Judiciary Committee Majority Staff Antitrust Report. Competition Policy International (https://www.competitionpoli cyinternational.com/understanding-the-house-judiciary -committee-majority-staff-antitrust-report/).

Kuran, T. (2011) *The Long Divergence: How Islamic Law Held Back the Middle East*. Princeton University Press.

Lagorio, C. (2016) Inside Airbnb's massive Olympics plans. *INC*, June (https://www.inc.com/christine-lagorio/airbnb-rio-oly mpic-plans.html).

Lamarck, J.-B. (1809) *Philosophie zoologique, ou exposition des considérations relatives à l'histoire naturelle des animaux.* (English edition: (1914) *Zoological Philosophy*, trans. H. S. R. Elliot (http://www.blc.arizona.edu/courses/schaffer/449/La marck/Lamarck%20Zoological%20Philosophy.pdf).)

Levitt, T. (1960) Marketing myopia. *Harvard Business Review* 38(4): 45–56.

Libecap, G. (1989) *Contracting for Property Rights*. New York: Cambridge University Press.

Lilico, A. and Sinclair, M. (2016) The cost of non-Europe in the shar ing economy. In *The Cost of Non-Europe in the Sharing Economy: Economic, Social and Legal Challenges and Opportunities*. Brus sels: European Parliamentary Research Service (http://www .europarl.europa.eu/RegData/etudes/STUD/2016/558777/ EPRS_STU%282016%29558777_EN.pdf).

Littlewood, M. (2018) Modesty and scepticism are needed to re-win the case for free markets. *Economic Affairs* 38(3): 444–46.

Local Government Association (2019) Young people today half as likely to get on nation's 'broken' housing ladder. 29 June (https://www.local.gov.uk/about/news/young-people-today -half-likely-get-nations-broken-housing-ladder).

Lomax, J. W. and Callen, T. S. (1990) The development of the build ing societies sector in the 1980s. *Bank of England Quarterly Bul letin* 30(4): 503–10 (https://www.bankofengland.co.uk/-/med ia/boe/files/quarterly-bulletin/1990/the-development-of -the-building-societies-sector-in-the-1980s.pdf).

Maclean, B. and Elkind, P. (2004) *The Smartest Guys in the Room: The Amazing Rise and Scandalous Fall of Enron.* New York: Portfolio Trade.

Majority Staff, House Judiciary Committee (2020) Investigation of competition in digital markets. US Government Printing Office (https://judiciary.house.gov/uploadedfiles/competitio n_in_digital_markets.pdf?utm_campaign=4493-519).

Manne, G. A. and Wright, J. D. (2011) Google and the limits of antitrust: the case against the case against Google. *Harvard Journal of Law and Public Policy* 34: 171–244.

Marx, K. (1867) *Capital.* In *Marx/Engels Selected Works*, Volume 1. Moscow: Progress Publisher (https://www.marxists.org/arch ive/marx/works/1867-c1/ch01.htm).

Marx, K. and Engels, F. (1848) [1969] *The Communist Manifesto.* In *Marx/Engels Selected Works*, Volume 1. Moscow: Progress Publishers (https://www.marxists.org/archive/marx/works/ 1848/communist-manifesto/ch01.htm).

Meade, J. E. (1952) External economies and diseconomies in a competitive situation. *Economic Journal* 62: 51–69.

Munger, M. C. (2008) Orange blossom special: externalities and the Coase Theorem. Econlib, Liberty Fund, Indianapolis, IN (http://www.econlib.org/library/Columns/y2008/Munger bees.html).

Munger, M. C. (2015) Coase and the 'sharing economy'. In *Forever Contemporary. The Economics of Ronald Coase* (ed. C. Veljanovski). London: Institute of Economic Affairs.

Munger, M. C. (2017) Permissionless innovation: the fuzzy idea that rules our lives. Learn Liberty (https://www.learnliberty. org/blog/permissionless-innovation-the-fuzzy-idea-that -rules-our-lives/).

Munger, M. C. (2018) *Tomorrow 3.0: Transaction Costs and the Sharing Economy.* Cambridge University Press.

Nastasi, V. (2020) Passage of Prop. 22 helps some of California's gig workers, but Assembly Bill 5 should be repealed. *Reason* (https://reason.org/commentary/passage-of-prop-22-helps-some-of-californias-gig-workers-but-assembly-bill-5-should-be-repealed/).

Neumark, D. and Shirley, P. (2021) Myth or measurement: what does the new minimum wage research say about minimum wages and job loss in the United States? National Bureau of Economic Research (US), Working Paper 28388, DOI 10.3386/w28388.

North, D. C. (1992) *Transaction Costs, Institutions, and Economic Performance.* San Francisco, CA: ICS Press.

Olson, M. (1984) *The Rise and Decline of Nations: Economic Growth, Stagflation, and Social Rigidities,* reprint edn. New Haven, CT: Yale University Press.

Parker, G. G. and Van Alstyne, M. W. (2005) Two-sided network effects: a theory of information product design. *Management Science* 51(10): 1494–504.

Pinsker, J. (2015) The covert world of people trying to edit Wikipedia – for pay. *The Atlantic* (https://www.theatlantic.com/business/archive/2015/08/wikipedia-editors-for-pay/393926/).

Pofeldt, E. (2019) California's new employment law is starting to crush freelancers. CNBC (https://www.cnbc.com/2019/12/11/californias-new-employment-law-is-starting-to-crush-freelancers.html).

Rambhia, A. (2016) Get connected to profit: embracing software propels growth in IoT era: device vendors must transform into software companies, or become obsolete. Frost and Sullivan 'White Paper': Gemalto (https://www.iot-now .com/2016/07/26/50316-get-connected-to-profit-embracing -software-propels-growth-in-iot-era/).

Rhodes, C. (2020) Manufacturing: statistics and policy. House of Commons, Briefing Paper 01942 (https://commonslibrary .parliament.uk/research-briefings/sn01942/).

Richman, B. D. and Macher, J. T. (2008) Transaction cost economics: an assessment of empirical research in the social sciences. *Business and Politics* 10: 1–63.

Rizzo, M. (1979) *Time, Uncertainty, and Disequilibrium: Exploration of Austrian Themes.* Washington, DC: Lexington Books.

Rochet, J.-C. and Tirole, J. (2003) Platform competition in two-sided markets. *Journal of the European Economic Association* 1(4): 990–1029.

Rousseau, J.-J. [1754] (1984) *A Discourse on Inequality.* New York: Penguin.

Schoenauer, N. (2003) *6,000 Years of Housing.* New York: W. W. Norton and Co.

Schumpeter, J. (1934) *The Theory of Economic Development: An Inquiry into Profits, Capital, Credit, Interest, and the Business Cycle.* Cambridge, MA: Harvard University Press.

Schumpeter, J. (1942) *Capitalism, Socialism, and Democracy.* New York: Harper.

Seibert, C. (2008) There's no such thing as a free parking space. *Policy* 24(2): 7–13.

Shackle, G. L. S. (1979) *Imagination and the Nature of Choice.* Edinburgh University Press.

Shirky, C. (2009) *Here Comes Everybody: The Power of Organizing Without Organizations.* New York: Penguin.

Smith, A. [1776] (1981) *An Inquiry into the Nature and Causes of the Wealth of Nations.* Indianapolis, IN: Liberty Fund.

Statista (2021) Market capitalization of the largest U.S. internet companies 2021 and market capitalization of largest U.S. social media companies 2021.

Stossel, J. (2017) Stop! You need a license for that! Reason blog (http://reason.com/blog/2017/08/01/stossel-stop-you-need-a-license-for-that).

Thierer, A. (2014) *Permissionless Innovation: The Continuing Case for Comprehensive Technological Freedom.* Arlington, VA: Mercatus Institute.

Wilkinson, E. and Willoughby, L. A. (trans.) (1967) *Friedrich Schiller, Letters on the Aesthetic Education of Man.* Oxford: Clarendon Press.

Williamson, O. E. (1975) *Markets and Hierarchies.* New York: Free Press.

Williamson, O. E. (1981) The economics of organization: the transaction cost approach. *American Journal of Sociology* 87(3): 548–77.

Williamson, O. E. (1985) *The Economic Institutions of Capitalism: Firms, Markets, Relational Contracting.* New York: Free Press.

Zuboff, S. (2019) *The Age of Surveillance Capitalism: The Fight for a Human Future at the New Frontier of Power.* New York: Public Affairs Press, Hatchett Book Group.

INDEX

ABOUT THE IEA

The Institute is a research and educational charity (No. CC 235 351), limited by guarantee. Its mission is to improve understanding of the fundamental institutions of a free society by analysing and expounding the role of markets in solving economic and social problems.

The IEA achieves its mission by:

- a high-quality publishing programme
- conferences, seminars, lectures and other events
- outreach to school and college students
- brokering media introductions and appearances

The IEA, which was established in 1955 by the late Sir Antony Fisher, is an educational charity, not a political organisation. It is independent of any political party or group and does not carry on activities intended to affect support for any political party or candidate in any election or referendum, or at any other time. It is financed by sales of publications, conference fees and voluntary donations.

In addition to its main series of publications, the IEA also publishes (jointly with the University of Buckingham), *Economic Affairs*.

The IEA is aided in its work by a distinguished international Academic Advisory Council and an eminent panel of Honorary Fellows. Together with other academics, they review prospective IEA publications, their comments being passed on anonymously to authors. All IEA papers are therefore subject to the same rigorous independent refereeing process as used by leading academic journals.

IEA publications enjoy widespread classroom use and course adoptions in schools and universities. They are also sold throughout the world and often translated/reprinted.

Since 1974 the IEA has helped to create a worldwide network of 100 similar institutions in over 70 countries. They are all independent but share the IEA's mission.

Views expressed in the IEA's publications are those of the authors, not those of the Institute (which has no corporate view), its Managing Trustees, Academic Advisory Council members or senior staff.

Members of the Institute's Academic Advisory Council, Honorary Fellows, Trustees and Staff are listed on the following page.

The Institute gratefully acknowledges financial support for its publications programme and other work from a generous benefaction by the late Professor Ronald Coase.

Other books recently published by the IEA include:

The Economics of International Development: Foreign Aid versus Freedom for the World's Poor
William Easterly
Readings in Political Economy 6; ISBN 978-0-255-36731-8; £7.50

Taxation, Government Spending and Economic Growth
Edited by Philip Booth
Hobart Paperback 184; ISBN 978-0-255-36734-9; £15.00

Universal Healthcare without the NHS: Towards a Patient-Centred Health System
Kristian Niemietz
Hobart Paperback 185; ISBN 978-0-255-36737-0; £10.00

Sea Change: How Markets and Property Rights Could Transform the Fishing Industry
Edited by Richard Wellings
Readings in Political Economy 7; ISBN 978-0-255-36740-0; £10.00

Working to Rule: The Damaging Economics of UK Employment Regulation
J. R. Shackleton
Hobart Paperback 186; ISBN 978-0-255-36743-1; £15.00

Education, War and Peace: The Surprising Success of Private Schools in War-Torn Countries
James Tooley and David Longfield
ISBN 978-0-255-36746-2; £10.00

Killjoys: A Critique of Paternalism
Christopher Snowdon
ISBN 978-0-255-36749-3; £12.50

Financial Stability without Central Banks
George Selgin, Kevin Dowd and Mathieu Bédard
ISBN 978-0-255-36752-3; £10.00

Against the Grain: Insights from an Economic Contrarian
Paul Ormerod
ISBN 978-0-255-36755-4; £15.00

Ayn Rand: An Introduction
Eamonn Butler
ISBN 978-0-255-36764-6; £12.50

Capitalism: An Introduction
Eamonn Butler
ISBN 978-0-255-36758-5; £12.50

Opting Out: Conscience and Cooperation in a Pluralistic Society
David S. Oderberg
ISBN 978-0-255-36761-5; £12.50

Getting the Measure of Money: A Critical Assessment of UK Monetary Indicators
Anthony J. Evans
ISBN 978-0-255-36767-7; £12.50

Socialism: The Failed Idea That Never Dies
Kristian Niemietz
ISBN 978-0-255-36770-7; £17.50

Top Dogs and Fat Cats: The Debate on High Pay
Edited by J. R. Shackleton
ISBN 978-0-255-36773-8; £15.00

School Choice around the World … And the Lessons We Can Learn
Edited by Pauline Dixon and Steve Humble
ISBN 978-0-255-36779-0; £15.00

School of Thought: 101 Great Liberal Thinkers
Eamonn Butler
ISBN 978-0-255-36776-9; £12.50

Raising the Roof: How to Solve the United Kingdom's Housing Crisis
Edited by Jacob Rees-Mogg and Radomir Tylecote
ISBN 978-0-255-36782-0; £12.50

How Many Light Bulbs Does It Take to Change the World?
Matt Ridley and Stephen Davies
ISBN 978-0-255-36785-1; £10.00

The Henry Fords of Healthcare: …Lessons the West Can Learn from the East
Nima Sanandaji
ISBN 978-0-255-36788-2; £10.00

An Introduction to Entrepreneurship
Eamonn Butler
ISBN 978-0-255-36794-3; £12.50

An Introduction to Democracy
Eamonn Butler
ISBN 978-0-255-36797-4; £12.50

Having Your Say: Threats to Free Speech in the 21st Century
Edited by J. R. Shackleton
ISBN 978-0-255-36800-1; £17.50

Other IEA publications

Comprehensive information on other publications and the wider work of the IEA can be found at www.iea.org.uk. To order any publication please see below.

Personal customers

Orders from personal customers should be directed to the IEA:

IEA
2 Lord North Street
FREEPOST LON10168
London SW1P 3YZ
Tel: 020 7799 8911, Fax: 020 7799 2137
Email: sales@iea.org.uk

Trade customers

All orders from the book trade should be directed to the IEA's distributor:

NBN International (IEA Orders)
Orders Dept.
NBN International
10 Thornbury Road
Plymouth PL6 7PP
Tel: 01752 202301, Fax: 01752 202333
Email: orders@nbninternational.com

IEA subscriptions

The IEA also offers a subscription service to its publications. For a single annual payment (currently £42.00 in the UK), subscribers receive every monograph the IEA publishes. For more information please contact:

Subscriptions
IEA
2 Lord North Street
FREEPOST LON10168
London SW1P 3YZ
Tel: 020 7799 8911, Fax: 020 7799 2137
Email: accounts@iea.org.uk